Mastering WooCommerce

Build complete e-commerce websites with WordPress and WooCommerce from scratch

Patrick Rauland

BIRMINGHAM - MUMBAI

Mastering WooCommerce 4

Copyright © 2020 Packt Publishing

Commissioning Editor: Pavan Ramchandani
Acquisition Editor: Karan Gupta
Content Development Editor: Aamir Ahmed
Senior Editor: Mohammed Yusuf Imaratwale
Technical Editor: Suwarna Patil
Copy Editor: Safis Editing
Project Coordinator: Manthan Patel
Proofreader: Safis Editing
Indexer: Tejal Daruwale Soni
Production Designer: Jyoti Chauhan

First published: March 2020

Production reference: 1270320

Published by Packt Publishing Ltd.
Livery Place
35 Livery Street
Birmingham
B3 2PB, UK.

ISBN 978-1-83882-283-5

`www.packt.com`

I need to start this book by saying thank you to everyone who believed in me. I've been fortunate to work at WooThemes, where they trusted me with WooCommerce; I've worked at Automattic and helped shape Woo from within a much larger company; and I also need to acknowledge LinkedIn Learning (formerly Lynda.com), where I first learned HTML and then began to teach e-commerce courses, including a few on WooCommerce. Thank you to all of my bosses and colleagues who believed in me, and helped me go above and beyond!

My family has always been supportive and nurturing. Thank you, mom and dad, for building an incredibly steady place to jump off from. You gave me the best leg up anyone could ask for. And even when projects didn't go well, you were there. To my partner, Ren – thank you for allowing me to sneak away on a weekend and write for a few hours. Time is important to both of us so I appreciate every second you give me for my projects, including this book.

– Patrick Rauland

Subscribe to our online digital library for full access to over 7,000 books and videos, as well as industry leading tools to help you plan your personal development and advance your career. For more information, please visit our website.

Why subscribe?

- Spend less time learning and more time coding with practical eBooks and Videos from over 4,000 industry professionals

- Improve your learning with Skill Plans built especially for you

- Get a free eBook or video every month

- Fully searchable for easy access to vital information

- Copy and paste, print, and bookmark content

Did you know that Packt offers eBook versions of every book published, with PDF and ePub files available? You can upgrade to the eBook version at www.packt.com and as a print book customer, you are entitled to a discount on the eBook copy. Get in touch with us at customercare@packtpub.com for more details.

At www.packt.com, you can also read a collection of free technical articles, sign up for a range of free newsletters, and receive exclusive discounts and offers on Packt books and eBooks.

Contributors

About the author

Patrick Rauland is obsessed with WooCommerce. He has used it as a customer, worked for WooCommerce support, developed core functionality in WooCommerce itself, led three releases, and helped plan their yearly conference (WooConf). He now helps people by writing his blog, creating courses for LinkedIn Learning/Lynda.com, and writing books. Patrick is also the co-founder of WooSesh, an online conference for WooCommerce developers and store owners. Patrick lives in Denver, Colorado, where you can probably find him at a local coffee shop, typing away.

I would like to acknowledge the team at Packt Publishing: without their talent and dedication, this book would not be what it is. In particular, I would like to thank Aamir Ahmed and Mohammed Yusuf Imaratwale for having faith in this book from the beginning. Adapting Aamir's many insightful comments and suggestions really helped lift the quality of this book, and I am grateful for all the time and effort he put into this book. I'd also like to thank the technical reviewer, Jeff Daigle, and the technical editors, for their thorough attention to the programming aspect of this book. Their detailed labels and understanding of target audiences, along with their invaluable comments, greatly improved the clarity of this book.

Finally, a special thanks to all of my students for all of their questions. You constantly challenged me to learn more and I'll always appreciate that.

About the reviewer

Jeff Daigle is an e-commerce consultant specializing in custom WooCommerce development for subscription- and membership-based sites. He has been building websites for 25 years, and started designing and developing with WordPress in 2006. His varied background in design, development, marketing, and project management helps him to understand complex business requirements and build elegant solutions for his clients. Jeff has been a featured speaker at WooConf, WooSesh, Lift Off Summit, and Makers Biz. He lives in Denver, Colorado, and he works with clients worldwide.

Packt is searching for authors like you

If you're interested in becoming an author for Packt, please visit `authors.packtpub.com` and apply today. We have worked with thousands of developers and tech professionals, just like you, to help them share their insight with the global tech community. You can make a general application, apply for a specific hot topic that we are recruiting an author for, or submit your own idea.

Table of Contents

Preface

WooCommerce is one of the most popular e-commerce platforms in the world. There are over 1,000,000 stores running WooCommerce for a huge variety of reasons. Some store owners like the thousands of themes they have access to, some like that they can build on top of their existing WordPress sites, and others really like the open source customizable angle and knowing that they can always read and customize the code any way they want. If you decide to build a store on WooCommerce, be prepared for an almost overwhelming amount of choice. Because it's so popular, you'll always have a lot of options in front of you.

Mastering WooCommerce 4 takes you from having absolutely nothing to having a fully functioning store. As the title of the book implies, we will go deep into WooCommerce and show you the basic options as well as some of the more advanced customizations. We'll do so in an orderly way, starting from the very beginning by setting up a test WordPress site and covering fundamental topics that we'll revisit throughout the rest of the book. Each chapter that follows will expand on the basics, allowing for a gentle progression curve that will allow almost any user to follow along. Each chapter will cover a new section of WooCommerce and thus can be seen as an independent unit, letting you tackle it separately from the others if you are already proficient in the other topics.

We'll first introduce you to the basics of WooCommerce and WordPress, which will help you develop and debug any issue. You will then learn how to create a simple product and optimize it for SEO. We will then look at shipping, taxes, and payment. After that, we will look into integrating with third-party services for fulfillment and reporting. Furthermore, we will also dive into **Point of Sale (POS)** systems that let you sell in person. We will then end the book by creating a very basic custom plugin that you can use for any customizations you wish to make.

Who this book is for

Mastering WooCommerce 4 is aimed at anyone who builds WooCommerce sites. You could be a developer who builds sites for clients or you could be a store owner who wants to take a DIY approach with your own store.

You should be familiar with the basics of WordPress. That means understanding what plugins do, what a theme does, how to install plugins and themes, how to keep your site up to date, and how to create posts and pages.

What this book covers

Chapter 1, *Installing WordPress and WooCommerce,* brings everyone up to speed. If you've never installed WooCommerce, we're going to go through it together step by step, looking at setting up our store settings, how we're going to accept payments, and how we're going to keep the admin interface clean.

Chapter 2, *Configuring Products,* digs into all of the settings for products. We'll cover when you should use certain product types, how to give your visitors as much information as possible, some of the premium product types such as WooCommerce Subscriptions, and when they are worth the money.

Chapter 3, *Organizing Products,* explains how to add categories and tags to your store and when you would want to do so. If you do it without thought, you're leaving money on the table. Organize your products in the correct way and customers will be able to find your products and check out in a flash.

Chapter 4, *Optimizing SEO and Attracting Traffic,* is all about getting traffic. We're going to look into some of the common ways to bring people to your site, focusing especially on **Search Engine Optimization (SEO)** and content marketing, which is very popular with WordPress.

Chapter 5, *Managing Sales through WP Admin,* helps store owners manage and fulfill sales. Once you get that traffic, you'll have orders and will need to ship your products. There are some hidden gems in the WooCommerce admin realm that make this process surprisingly easy.

Chapter 6, *Syncing Product Data,* illustrates how tricky it is to keep all of your product data in sync. We'll cover a manual process that you can use to update your products and investigate services that do this for you automatically.

Chapter 7, *Configuring In-Store POS Solutions,* will highlight the different ways you can sell products in person. We lay out several POS solutions, along with their benefits and drawbacks, to help you choose the right one for your store or your client's store.

Chapter 8, *Using Fulfillment Software,* draws together another suite of tools, this time focusing on fulfillment (getting a package to a customer's door). There are built-in options that are great for small orders but at a certain point, you'll want to switch to a separate solution to save you money and time.

Chapter 9, *Speeding Up Your Store,* highlights several ways in which you can speed up your store and talks about the importance of doing so. If your store is slow, no one will want to check out, so look into these techniques to speed up your store.

Chapter 10, *Setting Up Your Theme*, will show you my two favorite themes for WooCommerce and how you can set them up to display your products.

Chapter 11, *Customizing the Product Page*, is all about building that perfect product page. We'll look into 360-degree images, videos, and adding social proof.

Chapter 12, *Building a Landing Page*, will show you some key principles of good landing page design, how you can add e-commerce functionality to the landing page, and then how to A/B test and optimize that page.

Chapter 13, *Creating Plugins for WooCommerce*, is here for the developers. If you want to take advantage of WooCommerce's open source code, now is the time to write code to help you modify WooCommerce itself, customize an order status, build plugins, and integrate them.

To get the most out of this book

You will need to have a functioning WordPress site. Ideally, you should know how to create a test or development site, since many of our examples will change the frontend of your site and you don't want your visitors seeing a work-in-progress store.

I highly recommend that you always keep WordPress and WooCommerce in their latest versions, as well as all plugins and themes for that matter. The further you are behind the latest live version, the more things won't work. It's also helpful, but not necessary, to have familiarity with HTML, CSS, JavaScript, and PHP.

Software/hardware covered in the book	OS requirements
WordPress 5	Windows, macOS X, and Linux (any)
WooCommerce 4	Windows, macOS X, and Linux (any)

If you are using the digital version of this book, we advise you to type the code yourself or access the code via the GitHub repository (link available in the next section). Doing so will help you avoid any potential errors related to the copying/pasting of code.

Download the example code files

You can download the example code files for this book from your account at www.packt.com. If you purchased this book elsewhere, you can visit www.packtpub.com/support and register to have the files emailed directly to you.

You can download the code files by following these steps:

1. Log in or register at www.packt.com.
2. Select the **Support** tab.
3. Click on **Code Downloads**.
4. Enter the name of the book in the **Search** box and follow the onscreen instructions.

Once the file is downloaded, please make sure that you unzip or extract the folder using the latest version of:

- WinRAR/7-Zip for Windows
- Zipeg/iZip/UnRarX for Mac
- 7-Zip/PeaZip for Linux

The code bundle for the book is also hosted on GitHub at https://github.com/PacktPublishing/Mastering-WooCommerce-4. In case there's an update to the code, it will be updated on the existing GitHub repository.

We also have other code bundles from our rich catalog of books and videos available at https://github.com/PacktPublishing/. Check them out!

Conventions used

There are a number of text conventions used throughout this book.

CodeInText: Indicates code words in text, database table names, folder names, filenames, file extensions, pathnames, dummy URLs, user input, and Twitter handles. Here is an example: "You can pass in a $args array."

A block of code is set as follows:

```
// Check to make sure WooCommerce is active
 if ( in_array( 'woocommerce/woocommerce.php',
apply_filters('active_plugins', get_option('active_plugins')))) {
    ((our existing code))
 }
```

Bold: Indicates a new term, an important word, or words that you see onscreen. For example, words in menus or dialog boxes appear in the text like this. Here is an example: "And then click the **Features** tab."

Warnings or important notes appear like this.

 Tips and tricks appear like this.

Get in touch

Feedback from our readers is always welcome.

General feedback: If you have questions about any aspect of this book, mention the book title in the subject of your message and email us at customercare@packtpub.com.

Errata: Although we have taken every care to ensure the accuracy of our content, mistakes do happen. If you have found a mistake in this book, we would be grateful if you would report this to us. Please visit www.packtpub.com/support/errata, selecting your book, clicking on the Errata Submission Form link, and entering the details.

Piracy: If you come across any illegal copies of our works in any form on the Internet, we would be grateful if you would provide us with the location address or website name. Please contact us at copyright@packt.com with a link to the material.

If you are interested in becoming an author: If there is a topic that you have expertise in and you are interested in either writing or contributing to a book, please visit authors.packtpub.com.

Reviews

Please leave a review. Once you have read and used this book, why not leave a review on the site that you purchased it from? Potential readers can then see and use your unbiased opinion to make purchase decisions, we at Packt can understand what you think about our products, and our authors can see your feedback on their book. Thank you!

For more information about Packt, please visit packt.com.

Installing WordPress and WooCommerce

WooCommerce was designed as a WordPress plugin from its conception. Everything that WooCommerce has done is done on top of the WordPress platform. So, while this is a book about mastering WooCommerce, we can't start talking about WooCommerce until we make sure a few basic things are taken care of in your WordPress installation.

We're going to make sure your WordPress site is set up correctly and then install WooCommerce. To do that, we're going to look into the following:

- Why and how you should use test sites
- Creating an ad-free admin experience
- How to install WooCommerce
- Configuring settings through the WooCommerce welcome wizard

Once you've done all of the preceding, you'll have WooCommerce installed on a test site and you can start building your online store.

Let's first look at why and how we should use test sites with any WordPress installation.

Importance of test sites

If you've been a WordPress developer for a while, you're probably familiar with test sites. And while they're important in regular WordPress development, they're *critical* in WooCommerce development. The following screenshot shows what a website development process looks like:

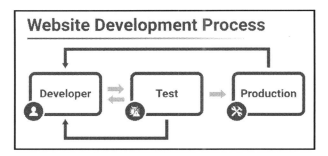

With a typical WordPress development project, you'll build custom functionality on your local machine. Then, you'll upload it to a test site where the client usually approves it. Then, you move the test site to the live site, replacing data and files.

And this works great for most WordPress projects. But when it comes to e-commerce, there are two problems:

- **You can never replace the live database**: Since an e-commerce site is always on and always accepting new orders, payments, and marking items as shipped, you can't replace the live database with the test database.
- **E-commerce functionality often needs a publicly accessible URL to work properly**: A lot of e-commerce functionality (shipping, payment, and taxes) interacts with third parties, some of which need a publicly accessible URL to return data. So, it's much harder to test your site on a local machine.

Since the e-commerce site has more demands, we're going to cover some of the things you need to do with a test site:

- Migrate files but not the database
- Test with a publicly accessible URL

With these two extra criteria met, both of which can be done by a good website host, you can easily test and launch your own WooCommerce site. Let's look into migrating files first.

Migrating the files but not the database

With any sort of e-commerce site, it's always on, and always accepting new orders and payments and marking items as shipped. Because of this, if you ever replace a live database with a test database, you could have catastrophic results. It will often take days or weeks to make a test site, test the changes, and get them approved. In that time frame, there will very often be a new order and if you replace the live database with the test database, you erase all records of that order. If you're lucky, there will still be an email sent to you and the customer but you'll have no other records, which is a bad spot to be in.

This is why you'll never want to overwrite the live database. You'll want to work with a host that can let you move your code to your live site and leave the live database intact. Or you'll want to have your own processes to quickly move all files from your test site to your live site.

There are a couple of hosts worth mentioning that have a really nice infrastructure that helps you to build great WooCommerce sites:

- WP Engine (`https://wpengine.com/`)
- Pantheon (`https://pantheon.io/`)
- Liquid Web (`https://www.liquidweb.com/`)

These hosts will be able to help you to migrate just the files you want without moving the database. If you want to use another host, just make sure they have the infrastructure to migrate files between a test and a live website.

And if you're wondering why I'm mentioning hosts instead of local development software, that's because it's important in e-commerce to develop sites with a publicly accessible URL.

Testing with a publicly accessible URL

When you're working on a WooCommerce site, you'll need to test *all* of the e-commerce functionality, such as getting shipping rates, importing tax rates, and accepting payment. Unfortunately, some of these third parties use legacy systems to deliver data to your site. And for some of these systems to work, they deliver data to your site via a publicly accessible URL. For example, a shipping company might return data to your store about a custom shipping price with a link similar to
this: `yourstore.com/?custom_parameter=foo`.

If they can't access your store via a URL, these services might not work. So, if you want to develop a custom theme or plugin that interacts with the cart or checkout, you might have to do that development on a test site instead of a local site on your own computer.

If you are doing a lot of custom development, it still saves time to develop on your local machine and when you want to test the site, move all of your local files to your test site. But for many e-commerce sites, you can save time by doing all of your development on a test site and skipping the local site.

Now that we know how to develop sites, let's make sure our admin is free from promotions.

Creating an ad-free experience

Both WooCommerce and Jetpack, a plugin we'll install later in this chapter, include promotions. And these promotions make it less clear what's going on. And if you're developing this site for a client, *you* want to recommend plugins—you don't want your plugin doing that for you.

As an example, in the following screenshot, there's a promotion for premium functionality:

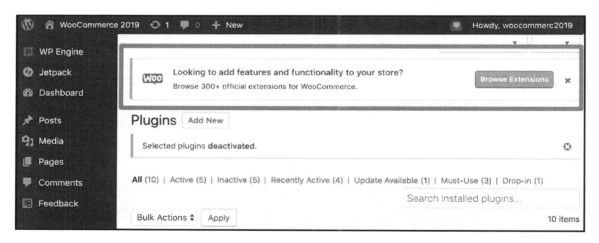

 Note: Throughout this book, I'll include several screenshots. To make sure these are valuable to you, I'm going to make sure they're showing you what I need you to see and I'll get rid of extra content.

To make this book clearer, I'm going to install two plugins that remove these ads, which lets me share more useful screenshots and will give you and your clients a much cleaner user experience.

Let's first install something to prevent promotions from Jetpack.

Jetpack Without Promotions

One of the plugins you can use to remove all of the ads in Jetpack is Jetpack Without Promotions. You can get this plugin from WordPress (`https://wordpress.org`). The following screenshot displays how it looks:

The actual code for this plugin is tiny. There are only a couple of important lines:

```
add_filter( 'can_display_jetpack_manage_notice', '__return_false', 20 );
add_filter( 'jetpack_just_in_time_msgs', '__return_false', 20 );
add_filter( 'jetpack_show_promotions', '__return_false', 20 );
```

The first line disables promotions for site management through WordPress (`https://jetpack.com/support/site-management/`).

The next line turns off *just in time* messages (`https://developer.jetpack.com/hooks/jetpack_just_in_time_msgs/`). These are not errors or warnings—those will still come through normally. Just-in-time messages are nudges to use free and paid features in Jetpack.

The final line turns off promotions in the plugin search results, which was added in Jetpack 7.1 (`https://wptavern.com/jetpack-7-1-adds-feature-suggestions-to-plugin-search-results`).

Surbma | WooCommerce Without Marketplace Suggestions

In WooCommerce 3.6, the WooCommerce team announced Marketplace Suggestions (https://woocommerce.wordpress.com/2019/04/03/extension-suggestions-in-3-6/). These inject recommendations for official WooCommerce extensions into the Orders screen and the Products screen for the store owner. They were adjusted just prior to the release and will likely evolve in the next few versions.

There's a plugin on the WordPress site called **Surbma | WooCommerce Without Marketplace Suggestions**, which disables these promotions, as shown here:

At the moment, there's only one important line in the plugin:

```
add_filter( 'woocommerce_allow_marketplace_suggestions', '__return_false'
);
```

The code to disable the promotions is quite simple: one filter that removes them completely.

Making your own custom plugin

Each of the preceding plugins does one small thing very well. I like to call these utility plugins since they do one thing perfectly. They don't have a user interface, and they don't have ads or premium features—they just work.

You could make your own custom plugin for WooCommerce and include the four lines of code from the preceding two plugins and have the same end result.

If you want to be able to use WooCommerce without ads getting in your way, you'll want to install these plugins or build your own. Talking about installing WooCommerce, let's quickly take a look at how to do that in the next section.

Installing WooCommerce

Let's get started by actually installing WooCommerce on our site. Perform the following given steps:

1. Search for `WooCommerce` under plugins in your admin menu:

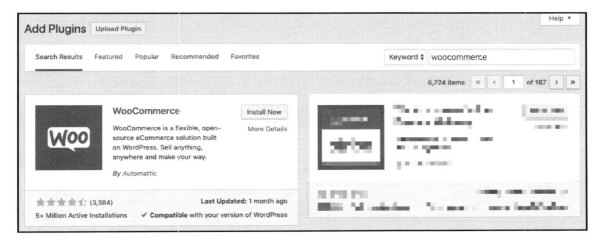

2. Click **Install Now** followed by **Activate**. This will take you to the welcome wizard, which will help you to configure all of the settings you'll need to get up and running.

Now we can configure the general settings in WooCommerce, followed by payment and then shipping.

General store settings

The first screen shows all of your general settings—things like where your store is located, what currency you accept, and what type of products you sell, which will set some smart defaults:

Go ahead and enter all of this information. One thing you should know about your address: WooCommerce assumes you have one location for your business. This should be your primary location. WooCommerce uses your location for two features:

- Calculating shipping rates via USPS, UPS, FedEx, and other shipping carriers
- Importing tax rates via WooCommerce Services

If you do have multiple locations, you'll have to configure a few extra settings in the shipping and tax settings sections.

There's also a setting for usage tracking. If you're running a live site, I recommend turning this on. It will give WooCommerce data about what plugins you're using, how many orders to have a month, and other data. This helps them to test against the most common plugins out there.

If you're running a local or test site, I recommend leaving this setting off since it will send data about a test installation. WooCommerce only wants data about live stores, not test scores, so we should leave the setting disabled on test stores.

Payment settings

The next step helps you to turn an online catalog into an online store by being able to take payment. In the settings here, make sure you can actually accept payment:

WooCommerce recommends two popular gateways:

- Stripe, which accepts credit cards and Apple Pay (`https://stripe.com/`).
- PayPal (Express), which accepts credit cards and PayPal balances (`https://wordpress.org/plugins/woocommerce-gateway-paypal-express-checkout/`).

There are hundreds of payment gateways available on WooCommerce and WordPress, and sometimes, you will want a specialized gateway for a specific currency, locale, or payment custom. However, many sites just want to accept credit cards or PayPal and these sites are perfect for Stripe and PayPal Express.

How many payment gateways

If you've never set up an e-commerce store, it might be confusing how many payment gateways you need. In short, you only need one payment gateway. However, it's possible for that payment gateway to go down, or more likely for a credit card to be declined, in which case, it's a great idea to have a backup payment gateway such as PayPal.

If you have the time, set up both payment gateways. If you only have time to set up one payment gateway, I'm a huge fan of Stripe since it's very easy to use and test without having to enter a bunch of information for a test account.

Installing plugins through the wizard

Depending on what options you choose, you might notice this little disclaimer at the bottom of the wizard:

> *The following plugins will be installed and activated for you:*
> *WooCommerce Stripe Gateway, WooCommerce Services, Jetpack,*
> *WooCommerce PayPal Checkout Gateway. Stripe and PayPal setup are powered by Jetpack and*
> *WooCommerce Services.*

This is notifying you that the wizard itself is installing plugins on your behalf. So, if you select Stripe, the free Stripe plugin from WordPress.org will be installed for you. Pretty great, right?

Just don't uninstall the plugin after the wizard just because you don't remember installing it.

Shipping settings

The next step is where you configure your shipping settings. These will likely be customized later with more detailed or powerful shipping features. But it's still worth setting up some basic shipping methods:

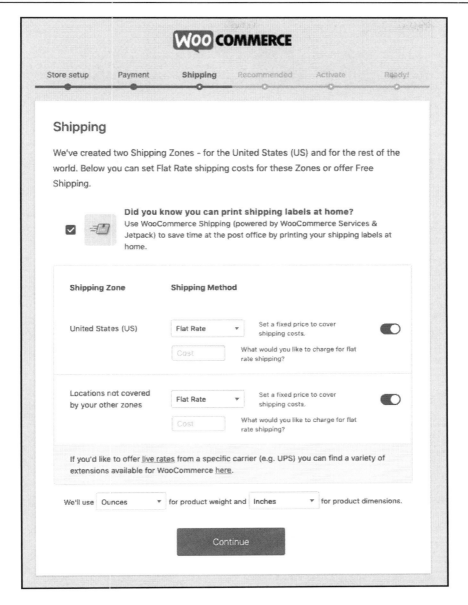

We have a few options here. We can configure our shipping methods within shipping zones, we can print labels at home, and we can choose our dimensions.

The most important thing to look into is the settings within the shipping zones.

Shipping zones

Before we get to the specific costs of shipping, it's helpful to know what WooCommerce means when they say **Shipping Zone**. A shipping zone is a group of countries, provinces or states, cities, and zip or postcodes. And each shipping zone can have its own set of shipping methods.

Check out these examples:

- I could offer free delivery in my home city.
- I could offer USPS inside the United States.
- I could offer FedEx everywhere else.

You can also have multiple methods within each shipping zone that the user selects, as in this example:

- Within the United States, I could offer USPS for all orders.
- And if you order over $50, I can offer 5-day free shipping with the option to still pick a faster USPS service.

We'll cover shipping in more detail later in this book. For now, just set a price for your country and a price for international shipping. You can also offer free shipping here.

Printing shipping labels

WooCommerce has a prechecked box for printing shipping labels at home. This requires both Jetpack and WooCommerce Services, which will be installed if they haven't been already.

For new store owners who have never shipped a package before, I recommend turning this off. For the first 5-10 orders, I think it makes more sense to physically drop off packages at the post office where you can see box sizes and packaging and ask questions.

Once the store owner has a handle on things and they know exactly how much things weigh and the box sizes, they need to go ahead and turn on this setting.

Dimensions

The last setting lets us choose our dimensions. WooCommerce will take a guess on what measurements we want to use based on our country. For our store, WooCommerce assumes we want to use ounces and inches, which will work fine. But if you need to, you can change your dimensions.

These will be used throughout WooCommerce. These dimensions will be used for packing items into boxes (with software called a box packer), calculating live shipping rates, and they're displayed on the product page, so you'll want to make sure they're correct here.

Recommendations

The next section is all about recommended add-ons for WooCommerce. Many of these make WooCommerce easier to use and integrate with third-party services. You can see the options here:

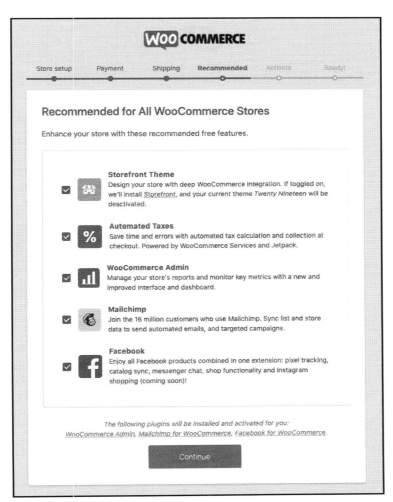

WooCommerce makes quite a few recommendations:

- **Storefront Theme** is a great theme that we'll be exploring. If you've never built an e-commerce store before, you'll want to use Storefront as a baseline for a good theme for e-commerce.
- **Automated Taxes** is another feature provided by WooCommerce Services. These will import tax rates (at the time of writing, only for the US) for you as soon as a customer goes through the checkout.
- **Mailchimp** is a fantastic freemium email newsletter service. This integration lets the users opt in to your newsletter as they go through the checkout.

The **Facebook** plugin is useful but not essential for stores. Users can already share any page they want. Checking this box gives you advanced functionality that you can always install later from WordPress.org. The one feature you might want immediately is pixel tracking. That's useful for any store that wants to use Facebook ads to help to generate a look-a-like audience on Facebook. But unless you're looking at doing ads in the near future or any of those advanced features, you don't need to install this plugin.

Activate

If any of the features you enabled require Jetpack or WooCommerce Services, you'll have to connect your store to WordPress, which is what powers Jetpack:

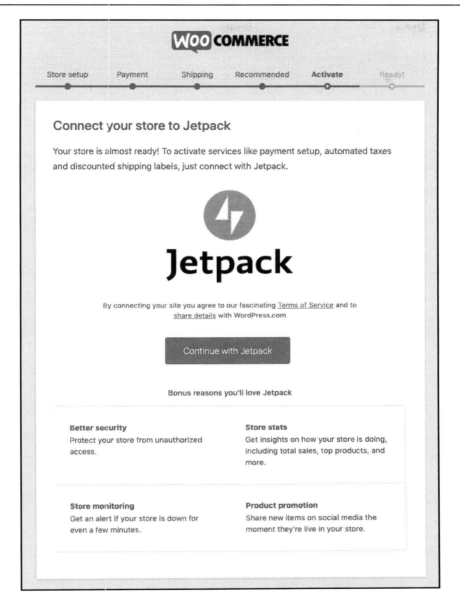

To do this, you need a publicly accessible site. You can use a local site and get any of these features. If you haven't done so yet, you can create a free WordPress account to connect your store.

Ready!

And with that, we're done! WooCommerce is ready to go and we can create our first product. The following screenshot shows the ready screen:

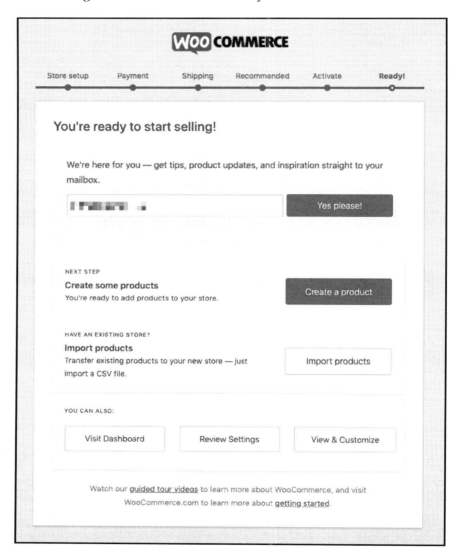

Now that we have installed and configured the WooCommerce plugin, let's see how to disable nags in the following section.

Disabling nags

There's one final thing we can do to make our experience in WooCommerce a little nicer. Click **View Dashboard** to get back to the WordPress administrator. You should see approximately four nags (depending on your store settings and what add-ons you installed) and one of those nags is *huge*. You can see the nags here:

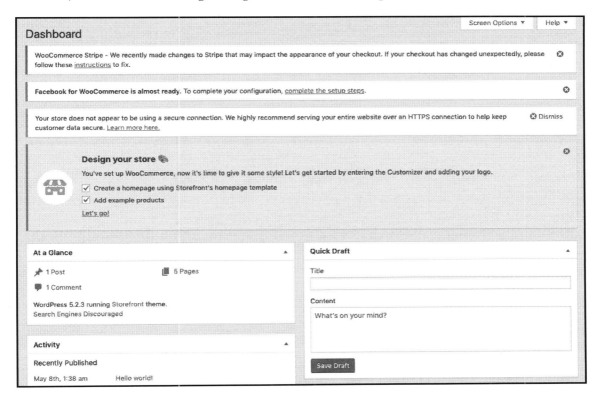

Let's temporarily disable the PayPal, Stripe, and Facebook plugins and switch back to a default theme. Here's our dashboard after disabling a few plugins:

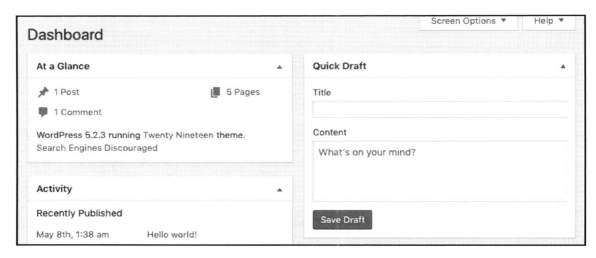

Switching to a default theme so we don't see storefront nags and disabling some payment gateways will temporarily remove the nags so you can actually see what you're doing in the administrator. This will make it much easier for you to follow along with this book and will give you a cleaner and easier user experience.

Don't worry—we'll continue customizing those plugins later in this book.

Summary

Before we could install WooCommerce, we had to make sure our WordPress site was set up correctly and that we could build everything in a properly setup test site.

Once we had that, we installed a few plugins to keep our admin interface free from ads. We then installed WooCommerce and Jetpack and configured a number of basic settings through the welcome wizard. With these steps, you can set up and test as many WooCommerce sites as you want.

Now that we've done all of that, we're ready to create products in our store. Configuring products will be covered in the next chapter.

Configuring Products 2

You can't have an online store without something to sell. Before we can sell something, we have to add products to our store. But before we do that, we have to know the different kinds of products you can add to your store.

We're going to look at three types of products that are included in the free WooCommerce plugin. We're also going to look at the Product Bundles (`https://www.woocommerce.com/products/product-bundles/`) and Subscriptions (`https://woocommerce.com/products/woocommerce-subscriptions/`) that are available through premium extensions on the WooCommerce website . Each of these types of products will have unique features, and choosing how you want to display your products in your store is an important decision.

In this chapter, we're going to look into the following:

- Simple products
- Variable products
- Digital products
- Product bundles
- Subscriptions

All of these product types build on each other. So, before you jump ahead and look into variable products, make sure to look at the section on simple products. By the end of this chapter, you should know what types of products you want to offer in your store as well as the technical information you need to configure them correctly.

Exploring the WordPress editor

Before we start adding products to our store, I want to point out one thing about the interface we're going to be using. This is the modern interface for editing posts and pages as of WordPress 5.0:

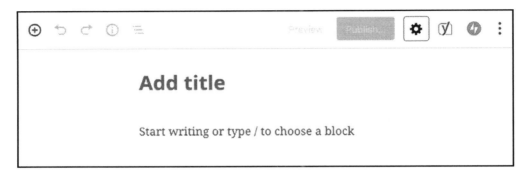

It's very clean and it uses the new block editor that comes with WordPress 5.0 called Gutenberg.

Simple products

The easiest type of product to create is unsurprisingly called a simple product. It's important to know how to create a simple product because everything else is based on it. So, you'll want to know exactly how to manipulate a simple product.

A good example of a simple product would be anything that comes in one format, such as a coffee cup, ring, or backpack. You can add a new product through your WordPress admin under **Products | Add New**.

We're going to look into a few different aspects of simple products:

- Required and optional fields—to add useful data to the product page
- Taxonomies (categories and tags)—to make it easy for users to browse through our store
- Images—to instantly communicate what our product looks like
- Description fields—to describe your products.

Product data fields

The only required field for a product is the **Product name** (also known as the title). If you add the product name to a product and publish it, you'll see an empty page:

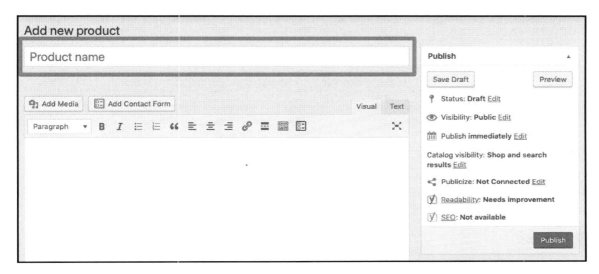

You can also add a price to the product. It can be 0 or any positive value. And as soon as you add a price, users can add it to their cart.

Optional fields

When you take a look at the add product screen, it might not be clear where you add all of the information about your products. You'll need to scroll down to see the **Product data** panel.

This controls the majority of the settings for your product, including the following:

- Product type (simple, variable, grouped, and so on)
- Downloadable and/or virtual
- Price
- Shipping dimensions
- Linked products

For now, leave the product type set to **Simple product**. Leave **Virtual** and **Downloadable** unchecked—we'll look at those later in this chapter.

Under the **Product data** panel, set a **Regular price** and a **Sale price**:

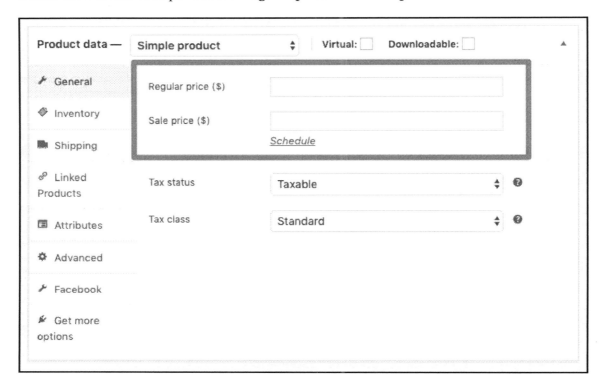

After setting a price, you will likely want to look into the inventory and stock settings. These track how much product you actually have in stock and they make sure that users can only check out while you have items in stock—a very handy tool for a store owner.

Inventory and stock

If you manage stock for your product, you can have WooCommerce track the quantities. Under **Product data | Inventory**, you can enter something for the following:

- Enter a value for **SKU** (Stock Keeping Unit), which is an ID for a product.
- Check **Manage stock**.
- Once **Manage stock** is checked, you can enter the **Stock quantity**.

I'm a big fan of setting the **Low stock threshold**, which will email you when your product is low in stock so you have enough time to order or produce more products.

Shipping

The **Shipping** tab in the **Product data** panel is important for two reasons:

- It's what your store uses to calculate live shipping rates.
- It's displayed to the customer on the frontend.

While images can be helpful to show the size and scale of products, nothing beats having dimensions listed on the product page. Consider the following example:

A friend of mine was looking to purchase a new refrigerator and did weeks of research. She found a great model and almost pressed the purchase button when she realized she had no idea of the size. She ended up purchasing a refrigerator from a different company and the original company lost out on $1,000+ sale because they didn't list their dimensions. So, don't forget to list dimensions!

There are two sets of shipping fields you'll want to fill in:

- **Weight**
- **Dimensions (Length, Width, and Height)**

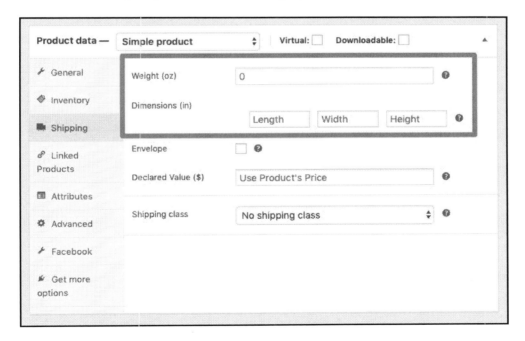

You'll need both of these for shipping quotes and they'll automatically appear on the frontend in an additional tab beneath the **Add to cart** button:

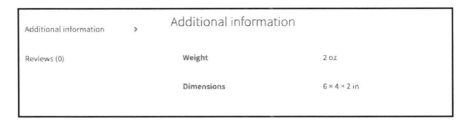

Once you get your shipping taken care of, it's important to make sure users can browse through your store and find your product. That's what taxonomies are for.

Understanding taxonomies

In addition to the **Product data** tab, you will likely want to organize your product with categories and tags. In WordPress, these are commonly known as **taxonomies** (`https://developer.wordpress.org/themes/basics/categories-tags-custom-taxonomies/`).

You can find taxonomies (**Product categories** and **Product tags**) in the sidebar:

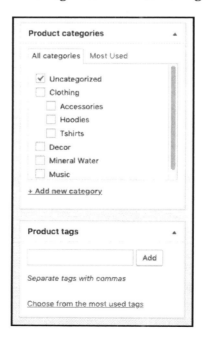

You typically add one product category and as many product tags as you want to your product. We'll get into maximizing categorization and how to best use categories and tags to help your visitors to navigate your store in the next chapter.

Once you add taxonomies and make your product easy to discover, we need to make sure that there's an image for your product. The image will tell users immediately what they're looking at and whether they should click for more details, so it's incredibly important.

Images

One thing you'll definitely want to look into are images for your product page. Images can instantly communicate what would take 1,000 words. And you can quite easily include dozens of images that engaged users will scroll through.

There are tons of articles on how valuable images can be to your store. Having multiple high-quality images that really show your product in detail and in context (for example, earrings shown on an ear) is crucial to your ability to sell online.

 To know more about the importance of images
visit: `https://baymard.com/blog/product-images-descriptive-text`

In WooCommerce, you can add as many images as you want using **Product image** and **Product gallery** in the sidebar:

The product image is the main image for the product and can be seen on the product page, in the cart, and on the shop page or any category pages.

The product gallery shows up on the product detail page. Users can see thumbnails, click to zoom in, and scroll through them with their arrow keys:

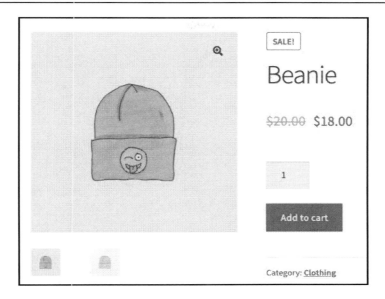

Let's see how to rename images for **Search Engine Optimization (SEO)** in the following section.

SEO tip for image filenames

We're going to cover SEO later in this book but there is one thing you can do now to prepare your site for better optimization. As you're uploading images to your site, make sure the image filenames make sense.

Filenames such as IMG1234.jpg don't tell search engines anything. If you can rename your image filenames to something that provides context to search engines, this will give you a small SEO boost, as in these examples:

- black-coffee-cup.jpg
- rainbox-umbrella.jpg
- 48-inch-{brand-name}-tv.jpg

We'll continue to optimize our products later in this book, but naming your images before you upload them will save you a ton of time.

Long and short descriptions

In addition to all of the product data, there's the main content area, which is known as the long description:

And there's a panel beneath the product data for the **Product short description**:

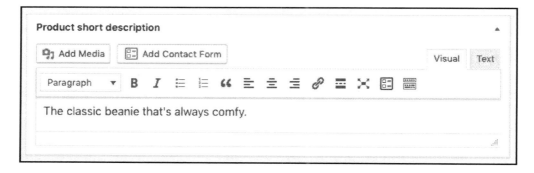

Both of these appear on the product page. The short description is a 1-2 sentence description of the product and appears above the fold on most themes and browsers.

The long description is where you put every detail you can. Most users won't read this but users who do will want to see complete information. Feel free to add paragraphs of content. Break it up with bold phrases and bullet points. You can even add images and headings.

A fully configured simple product

Once you've filled out all of the fields, publish your product and take a look at the resulting product page. The little pieces of information make a really compelling product page:

Now that we've looked into the settings for a simple product, let's take what we've learned, change a couple of fields, and give users a few choices on the product page.

Variable products

Simple products such as coffee cups and umbrellas are great, but many products have some variation. Posters come in multiple sizes, phone cases come in multiple colours, and clothes come in sizes and colours. For these types of products, we have variable products (https:/
/docs.woocommerce.com/document/variable-product/).

We're going to build on what we learned in the last section and we're going to look into a few concepts specific to variations:

- **Attributes**: These describe our products, for example, size or colour.
- **Variations**: These are options our users select, for example, a small t-shirt.
- **Images for variation**: These are uploaded differently than simple products.
- **Multi-attribute products**: These are for configuring multiple attributes in the backend (for example, size and colour).
- **Troubleshooting variations**: This is for what to do when something isn't working.

The first thing we have to do is select **Variable product** at the top of the **Product data** panel:

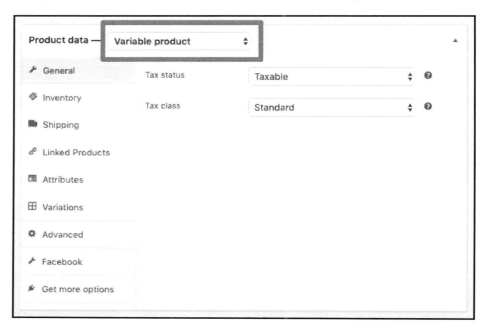

In many ways, variable products are configured exactly like simple products but the information in the backend is slightly rearranged.

Attributes

To be able to select what you want in a product, WooCommerce has to know what the options are. These options are called **attributes** and they can be found in **Product data** | **Attributes**:

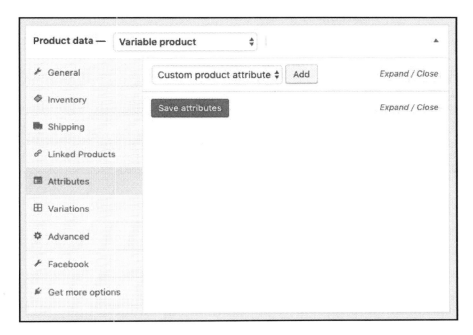

There are two types of attributes:

- **Custom product attribute**
- **Global attribute**

Functionally speaking, they're almost identical. The biggest difference is that global attributes can be reused between products where custom product attributes have to be created for each product, which means a lot less typing on your end.

Another difference is that global product attributes can be used for filtering. So, if you have filters on the shop page to help users to navigate your products, you can filter by specific attributes and this can only be done with global product attributes. If you have a product with unique attributes that no other product will have, then it's convenient to use the custom product attributes:

1. Let's add a global product attribute under **Products | Attributes**.
2. Add a **Name** for the attribute. The attribute is the name of the categorization, for example, colours, sizes, and cuts—not red, small, or v-neck:

Attributes

Add new attribute

Attributes let you define extra product data, such as size or color. You can use these attributes in the shop sidebar using the "layered nav" widgets.

Name

Name for the attribute (shown on the front-end).

Slug

Unique slug/reference for the attribute; must be no more than 28 characters.

☐ Enable Archives?

Enable this if you want this attribute to have product archives in your store.

Default sort order

Custom ordering ↕

Determines the sort order of the terms on the frontend shop product pages. If using custom ordering, you can drag and drop the terms in this attribute.

Add attribute

3. Then, click on **Configure terms**. This will let you configure individual values.

4. Now, go ahead and add your values, for example, Red, Blue, and Green:

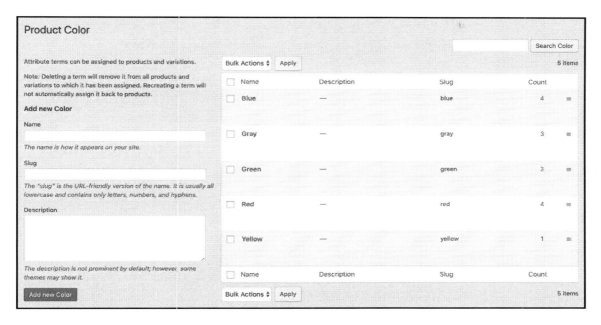

Now, let's take a look at variations for the products.

Variations

Now that we've added attributes, we can use them to create variations. To do so, follow these steps:

1. Refresh your edit product page. Then, go to **Product data** | **Attributes**.
2. Select your attribute from the drop-down menu and click **Add**.
3. You can select your values. If you have clothes that generally come in small, medium, large, and extra large, you might have a particular item that only comes in small and medium. In that case, just select small and medium:

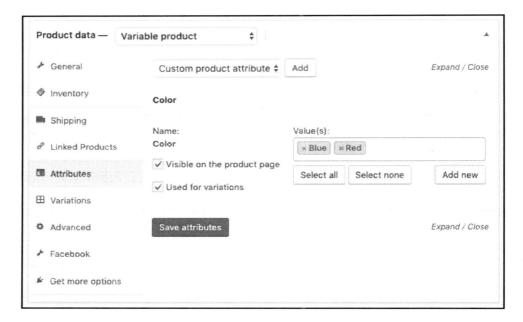

4. Make sure you check **Used for variations**.
5. Click **Save attributes**.
6. Click on the **Variations** tab in the **Product data** panel. From here, you can add individual variations. In the drop-down menu, select **Add variation**:

Editing individual variations

Once you have a variation, you can click into it and see per-variation settings. Fields such as **Regular price ($)**, **Sale price ($)**, **SKU**, inventory, and images are all very easy to customize via variation:

You can add as many variations as you want, although for maintenance purposes as well as clarity I try not to have too many options.

When you're done with each variation, make sure to click **Save changes**, and when you're done editing the product, click **Update**.

I've gone ahead and created two variations. Here's what they look like on the frontend:

And here's the same product once we've selected a different option from the drop-down menu:

Let's get started with variations in the next section.

Images for variations

Before we move forward, I want to highlight one aspect that's a little confusing about variations. You can have variations, each with their own unique product image. To do this, follow these steps:

1. In the backend under **Variations**, you can select an image:

2. Then, select that variation via drop-down menus; you'll see the image replace the main product image.

This is one of the most useful application variations as you can show people what they're going to get with each variation.

Multi-attribute variations

Some products have multiple attributes. A good example is clothing that could come in different colours and sizes.

You follow the preceding steps in the *Attributes* and *Variations* sections, except instead of adding one attribute, you add multiple attributes and make sure they're all used for variations.

With clothing that has a different image for each colour, we can create a variation for each colour and for the size, we can set **Any Size**:

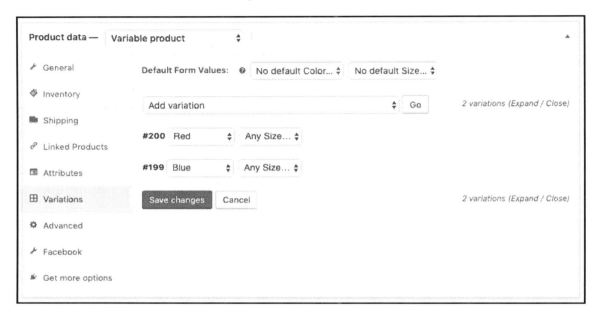

When a user selects the size and colour, the main image will be replaced and users can add the item to their cart.

Troubleshooting variations

If you ever notice that you don't see the **Add to cart** button on the frontend after selecting options in drop-down menus, there's very likely something going on wrong with your site.

Since the variations functionality uses JavaScript, it's often a JavaScript error that's preventing product variations from working correctly. It's very likely an error in your theme or one of your plugins.

Using a test site, disable all of your plugins and switch to a default theme and you should see the issue go away. Then, switch your theme back on and see whether the issue persists. If it doesn't appear, turn on your plugins one by one until you see the issue. Then, you know which plugin is responsible and you can reach out to the developer for support.

Digital products

Many store owners sell physical products such as shirts and mugs. But you can also sell downloadable files and virtual products such as memberships. For this, WooCommerce lets you modify a product and give it additional settings.

Digital products aren't a separate type of product (such as simple or variable)—they're a modifier: something you can add on to your simple or variable product. And the new fields will appear in slightly different places depending on the type of product. I'll be showing a simple product with digital fields. If you want to create a variable product with digital fields, the settings will be almost identical but under the **Variation** settings instead of the **General** tab.

Digital products

Before we change settings, we need to define terms. WooCommerce uses specific terms with specific meanings. You can make a product virtual and/or downloadable:

Let's see what these options mean:

- **Virtual** means the product has no physical presence. Therefore, it won't be shipped and the shipping tab will disappear. And if an order contains exclusively virtual products, the customer will skip the shipping section of the checkout.
- **Downloadable** means the product has downloadable files. There will be additional fields for the downloads. And the customer will automatically be emailed these files after payment is complete.

Downloadable but not virtual

Something I get asked all the time is: *Can a product be downloadable but not virtual?*

Yes! That's exactly why these are two different settings. A good example would be ordering both a physical CD or DVD, which will be shipped, and an immediate download. In that case, you need to deliver files (downloadable) and you need shipping details (not virtual).

Other good examples would be the following:

- Installation instructions
- FAQs
- Bonus content

Configuring virtual and downloadable products

Configuring a virtual product couldn't be easier. Just check the **Virtual** setting at the top of the **Product data** panel.

Downloadable products are a little more work than virtual. Let's start by checking the **Downloadable** setting at the top of the **Product data** panel.

Under the **General** tab of the **Product data** panel, you'll see a few new fields:

You can add as many files as you want. Give each one a name and link to the file or upload a file.

Are downloadable files safe?

Some store owners worry about uploading files to their site. WooCommerce uses a few different technologies to prevent users from pirating your files (https://docs. woocommerce.com/document/digital-downloadable-product-handling/).

In addition, any files you upload will be hidden from search engines.

For the most part, it isn't worth a ton of effort to prevent piracy. If a user really wants to pirate your content, they'll find a way to do so. But you can always limit downloads and add an expiry time.

One way to protect PDF is with PDF stamping (https://woocommerce.com/products/ woocommerce-pdf-watermark/). This embeds personal user information in the PDF (in very small, hard-to-notice print). This way, you have some idea of who shared the original document. This PDF stamping product is a premium plugin, but there are also free solutions on the market.

Large downloadable files

Most web servers have enough space to host files such as desktop wallpapers, PDFs, and images. But if you have a lot of files or if you have large files, then you'll want to find a host for these files. This will speed up your site and could reduce your hosting costs.

Amazon S3 is one of the best tools for sharing static assets such as PDFs, images, and media files. And there's a fairly inexpensive plugin from WooCommerce called Amazon S3 Storage that integrates Amazon S3 with your store (https://woocommerce.com/products/ amazon-s3-storage/).

You can also link to Dropbox or any other file storage program you want, although those methods are slightly less secure.

Accessing downloads

Once a user has purchased a downloadable product, they'll see a link to download the file(s) on the **Order received** page:

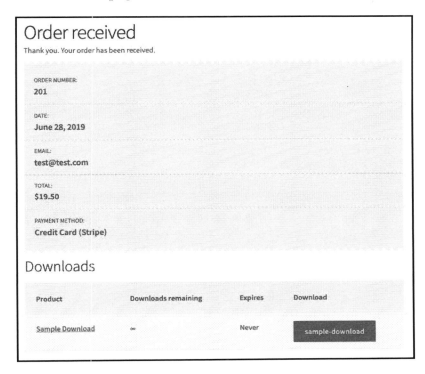

And they'll also see the information in an email from WooCommerce as well as under **My Account** on your site. So, there are multiple places where the user can find their downloads.

PayPal and downloads

If you're using PayPal Standard (included in WooCommerce) for payment, there's a slight delay with the PayPal IPN and customers won't see their downloads until payment is confirmed.

See WooCommerce's advice on how to handle this: `https://docs.woocommerce.com/document/digital-downloadable-product-handling/#section-12.`

Exploring Product Bundles

One of the best ways to sell more, or help your clients to sell more, is to bundle your products. In WooCommerce, there's a freeway that's built-in and an extension that makes it a much easier process. We'll look at both.

Grouped products

In addition to simple products and variable products, you can also make a **Grouped product**:

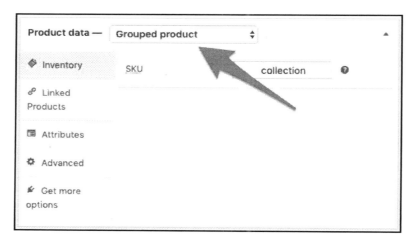

A grouped product is a collection of products that a user can select from one page. A good example of this would be products on a special sale.

When you make a product a grouped product, this will remove the **General** and **Shipping** tabs.

To add products to a grouped product, go to the **Linked Products** tab and notice the new **Grouped products** field. This field autocompletes previously created products:

Add a few to your grouped product and then take a look at the frontend. It can be seen in the following screenshot:

Grouped products are fine for a brand new store but most stores will want something a bit more robust—something that lets you bundle products into one package instead of an à la carte system where you are really just highlighting products.

Product Bundles

WooCommerce offers an extension called Product Bundles (`https://woocommerce.com/products/product-bundles/`), which lets you create a group of your existing products and you sell them as a group.

Once you install the extension, you'll see a new option in the drop-down menu on the edit product page. Select **Bundled Products** and you'll see a new tab appear in the **Product data** panel:

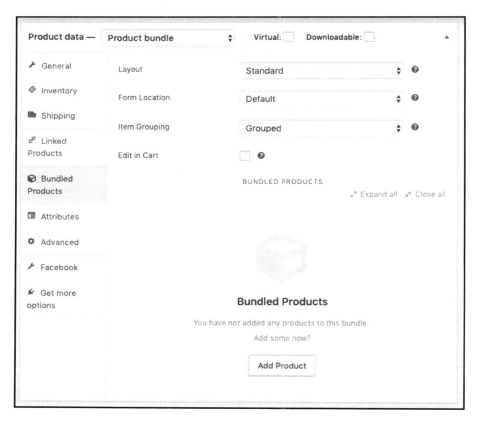

On this tab, there are several new settings:

- **Layout**
- **Form Location**
- **Item Grouping**
- **Edit in Cart**

And at the bottom, you can add products to the bundle. The one setting you might want to change is the **Layout** field. This will change how the bundled products appear on the product page. All of the options are useful but for our store, I'm going to select **Grid**.

Click **Add Product** and use the auto-suggest field to add a product to your bundle. Once you add a product to the bundle, you'll see options just for that product:

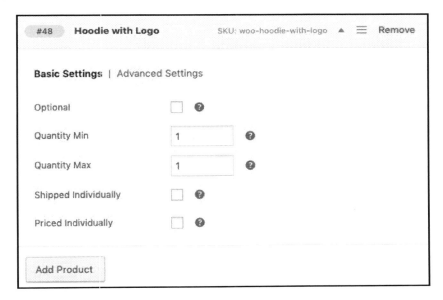

The defaults for this plugin are pretty smart and you don't have to make any changes.

In my case, I want to sell a bundle of three products together. I'll add the rest of the products, add a price under the **General** tab, and then view the frontend:

In the next section, we will learn about configurable bundles.

Configurable bundles

I like simple bundles but you can also give users options. You can let them customize the number of items in the bundle with minimums and maximums.

Let's say we want to have a bundle where we offer a t-shirt and hoodie and we let users buy a beanie if they want.

We can change the minimum quantity of the beanie to 0 and the maximum quantities to 5. Then, we can enable the **Optional** and **Priced Individually** checkboxes:

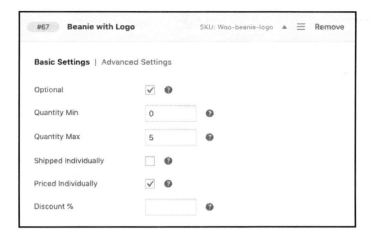

When we check **Priced Individually**, a new **Discount** field appears. You can use this to provide a discount on this product for being in the bundle.

This will work great but we can do more for the appearance. On the **Bundles** tab, change the **Layout** field to **Tabular** and now we can see it's a bit easier to edit quantities:

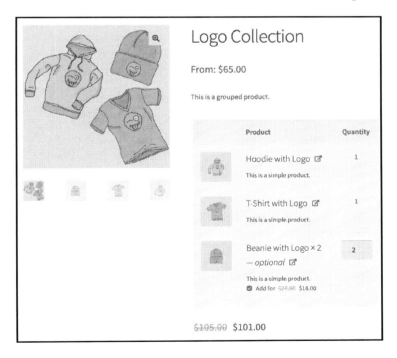

Let's learn about product kits in the next section.

Product kits

Most stores will use bundles at some point, which is why I wanted to show off the Product Bundles feature. I wanted to mention product kitting, which is where you select an item from bucket 1, an item from bucket 2, and an item from bucket 3 and put them all together.

This can be achieved with WooCommerce with an extension called Composite Products (`https://woocommerce.com/products/composite-products/`). But since a relatively small number of stores have products like that, I don't want to use valuable page space and instead, I recommend you refer to the official product page and documentation.

Subscriptions

The cost to get a new customer (acquisition cost) is pretty high. Many e-commerce stores only make a tiny profit on the first transaction because you often spend money attracting that customer with ads, tradeshows, and so on. That's why lots of store owners love recurring payments, where customers pay every week, month, or year.

WooCommerce Subscriptions (`https://woocommerce.com/products/woocommerce-subscriptions/`) is one of the most powerful subscription products on the market with all sorts of advanced features, such as the following:

- Pausing subscriptions
- Prorating subscriptions
- Synchronized payments

Creating a subscription product

To create a subscription product, you first have to purchase and install the WooCommerce Subscriptions extension. Once you do, you'll see a new option on the edit product page.

Select **Simple subscription** although you can also choose **Variable subscription**, which is very similar to variable products. When you select a subscription product, you'll see new fields:

As you can see, there are a ton of options. You can select the following:

- How often you want to bill people (weekly, bi-weekly, monthly, yearly, twice annually, and so on)
- When the subscription should expire—if ever
- Whether there's a free trial or conversely whether there's a signup fee
- Of course, a price

When you take a look at the frontend, the interface has totally changed to show all of our options to the visitor:

Let's see how to add a recurring payment option for the users in the following section.

Adding a recurring payment option to a product

If you've been to Amazon.com or other big online retailers, they will often offer a "subscribe and save" option for one-off purchases.

This lets users buy a product one time or if it is something they buy regularly, they can subscribe and save some money—and the retailer has consistent sales coming in.

And you can do this with your WooCommerce store with All Products for WooCommerce Subscriptions (https://woocommerce.com/products/all-products-for-woocommerce-subscriptions/), which is another paid extension by WooCommerce. You can turn any product into a subscription, as shown in the following screenshot:

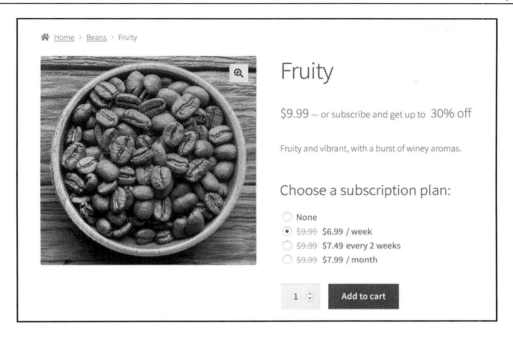

Let's get started with subscription settings in the following section.

Subscription settings

Subscriptions are complex and have their own settings page. Under **WooCommerce |
Settings | Subscriptions**, you can find a ton of settings.

Manual versus automatic renewals

If you live in the US, Canada, or Europe, you should have access to modern gateways that
save credit card numbers for you and give you a token so you can charge credit cards.

 WooCommerce has a list of subscription compatible gateways on their
site, here is the link if you want to take a quick look: `https://docs.`
`woocommerce.com/document/subscriptions/payment-gateways/`

That's all subscriptions need to automatically charge someone's card. But if you live outside of those areas, or if you are having a hard time finding the right payment gateway, you might not be able to get credit card tokens and bill someone on a recurring basis automatically. In that case, there's a feature called **Manual Renewals** that you can enable:

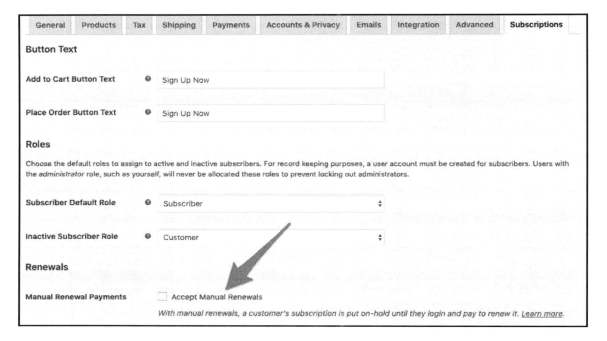

Users who have manual renewals will receive an email and will have to click a link and pay for an order every month. It's much more work for the end-user and is only designed for stores that can't get access to modern payment gateways.

If you have a modern gateway, there's a very good chance you don't want to turn on this feature.

Subscription switching

If you have a bunch of related subscriptions, you might want to enable subscription switching. For example, let's say every month, you deliver a 24-pack of soda. If the subscriber starts to overflow with soda rather than cancel, give them a smaller soda pack and a smaller discount so they stay subscribed and can upgrade in future months:

Switching

Allow subscribers to switch (upgrade or downgrade) between different subscriptions. Learn more.

Allow Switching   ✓ Never
                       Between Subscription Variations
                       Between Grouped Subscriptions
Synchronisation   Between Both Variations & Grouped Subscriptions

Align subscription renewal to a specific day of the week, month or year. For example, the first day of the month. Learn more.

Synchronise renewals   ☐ Align Subscription Renewal Day

I'm a big fan of enabling subscription switching between variations, but you can also enable them between a group of subscription products.

Synchronization

Some subscription stores do everything on a schedule. As an example, I subscribe to The Simple Jar. They deliver food weekly on a Monday.

They get all orders on Thursday, prep them on Sunday, and deliver on Monday morning. For businesses like this, for example, monthly loot boxes, that have a particular schedule, synchronizing subscriptions is hugely helpful. Customers can subscribe whenever and they'll get the next shipment and their payment will be postponed until the next billing cycle.

Check the **Align Subscription Renewal Day** checkbox and then follow the instructions under **Learn More** to enable this feature.

Retrying failed payments

Lastly, there's one other feature that's worth mentioning. Credit card numbers change and payments fail. Subscriptions have a feature that (under some conditions) will retry failed payments (`https://docs.woocommerce.com/document/subscriptions/failed-payment-retry/`). This gives credit cardholders time to pay off their balance.

Once you start getting the occasionally failed payment, ask your audience if this is something they'd want, and if so, you can enable it in your settings:

Retry Failed Payments	✓ Enable automatic retry of failed recurring payments
	Attempt to recover recurring revenue that would otherwise be lost due to payment methods being declined only temporarily. Learn more.

These are some of the settings every store owner and manager needs to know for WooCommerce. You should be able to create most product types and do so in such a way that customers are excited to see and purchase your product.

Summary

Listing products on your site is the first major hurdle for new store owners. Now that we know the pros and cons as well as the technical requirements of simple products, variable products, bundles, and subscriptions as well as how to add downloadable files to each of them, we can start adding them to our site.

Once we've added products to our store, we've turned our site from a brochure site to an online catalog. That's halfway to a full online store.

Now that you know how and why to add different types of products to your store, we can look into how to present these products to users so they can find the right product and add them to their cart in the next chapter.

3
Organizing Products

Once you've added products to your store, it's time to start thinking about the organization of your store. WooCommerce automatically lists products on your Shop page and if you're new to e-commerce, you might decide that's enough and stop there.

But there's actually a lot you can do to improve the organization of your store. And this organization can have a huge impact on the revenue the store generates.

As an example, in 2017, WooCommerce updated the category structure on its site. It reorganized 17 top-level categories into 7 top-level categories with subcategories as shown in the following screenshot:

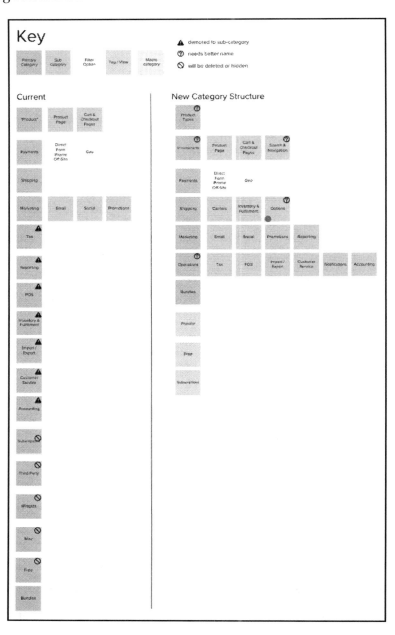

This one change improved the conversion rate of anyone landing on a category page by 20%. That's a *massive* improvement. And what's great is this helps both the store owner by getting more revenue and helps the user by making it easier to find the information they need.

Having a great structure for your store will also naturally help with your search engine optimization and drive more people to your category pages. Hopefully, now you understand how powerful it can be to properly organize your products.

In this chapter, we're going to cover the various ways you can organize your products, including the following:

- Categorizing and tagging
- Optimizing product archive pages
- Adding product filters to your Shop page
- Using product blocks through your site

Let's start with categorization and tagging.

Categorizing and tagging

First, let's talk about what's possible with two of the most commonly used WooCommerce organizational tools: categories and tags. Each product in WooCommerce can have categories and tags. Categories tend to be hierarchical while tags have a flat structure. It's a best practice to have one category and several tags.

Here's an example product's category and you could add tags right below:

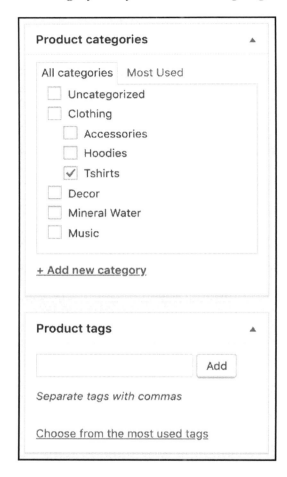

You might notice that you *can* add multiple categories to a product but that doesn't mean you *should*. I recommend you only use *one* category for each product. WooCommerce with the Storefront theme and a few other themes has a really nice breadcrumb feature that shows users where they are in the catalog. This won't work well with multiple categories.

You can see the breadcrumbs in the following screenshot:

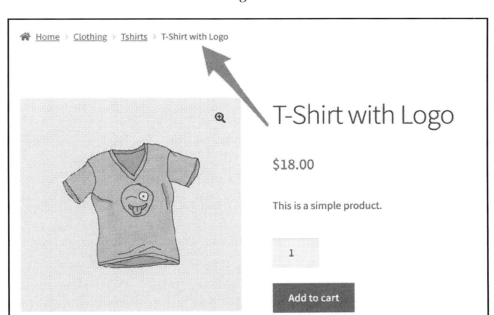

The breadcrumb feature on the product page lets users easily navigate to parent categories or all of the way back to the Shop page.

To make categories useful to your users, you'll want to make sure they're clearly named and understood and there's no ambiguity. To do that, I use a strategy called *mutually exclusive and collectively exhaustive*.

Mutually exclusive and collectively exhaustive

To help users to navigate your store, you have to have a well-designed category structure. And the phrase I always use is that categories have to be **mutually exclusive and collectively exhaustive**.

Mutually exclusive means categories shouldn't overlap each other. So, each item should fit clearly into only one category.

Collectively exhaustive means there should be a category for every type of product you sell. You don't want to have products that are not in a category and you want to try to avoid categories such as *Other* or *Miscellaneous* since shoppers rarely click these.

So, for the preceding screenshot, a good set of categories would be these:

- T-shirts
- Hoodies
- Accessories

And a bad set of categories would be these:

- Smiley faces
- Blue apparel
- V-necks
- Miscellaneous

All of these categories overlap with each other and store owners will be tempted to put the product in multiple categories, which is confusing to users. As a store builder, you'll want to make sure that none of your categories overlap with one another and you'll make a structure that makes sense to users, which will help your store to make more sales.

Once you have a solid set of categories, you'll want to add a few tags to your product.

Tagging products

Now that we have a system for categorizing products, we need a system for tagging products. There's a temptation to make the tagging structure similar to the category structure.

A store in my local area that happens to use WooCommerce has a category and tag structure that looks like the following screenshot:

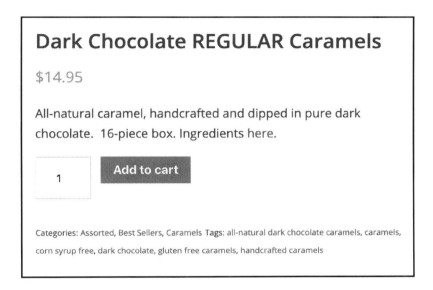

Do you see anything confusing for the user about this structure? If I want to browse by caramel chocolates, what do I click?

- **Categories | Caramels**
- **Tags | Caramels**

This is actually a common issue. Many store owners have a tag structure that's too similar to product categories. And both users, as well as search engines, get confused. You want to make sure it's 100% obvious what the user should click on. This will increase those conversion rates.

What I recommend is to use one system for categories and a completely different system for tags. So, going back to clothing, I might use the following as categories:

- T-shirts
- Hoodies
- Accessories

And these would be good tags to navigate between the categories:

- Smiley faces
- Blue apparel

When your client comes to you with 100 categories and no subcategories, now you know better. Customers will find that hard to navigate, and your client's store might fail. You now know how to clearly categorize and tag your store to help users to find the right products so the store can make more money.

Once we have that structure in place, it's time to optimize the product archive pages.

Optimizing product archive pages

Now that we have intuitive categories our users can browse, let's optimize these pages. We can make them much easier to read for the user, which will also help search engines understand what this page is for and hopefully increase the amount of traffic they send to these pages. We're going to do the following:

- Write descriptions for the product category pages to help both users and search engines.
- Edit our URLs so they're clean and easy to read.

When we're done with this section, users will understand the product archive pages (category pages) and you should get more inbound traffic to your store.

Write descriptions for product categories

One of the most important things you should do is add a description to your product category pages. To do that, follow the steps given here:

1. You can do this in WooCommerce in the backend through **Products | Categories | {{pick a category}}**:

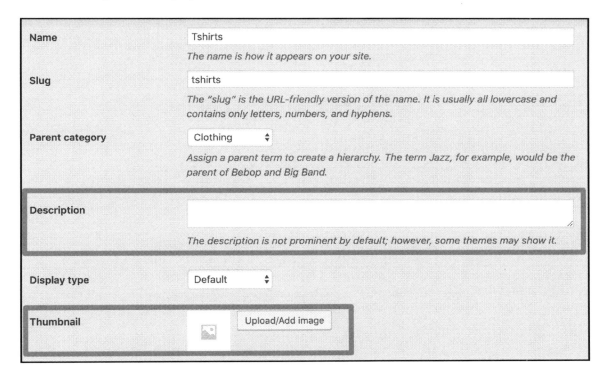

You can customize several details on this page including the category description and the thumbnail.

2. From here, you can write a description and upload a thumbnail for your category, as shown in this screenshot:

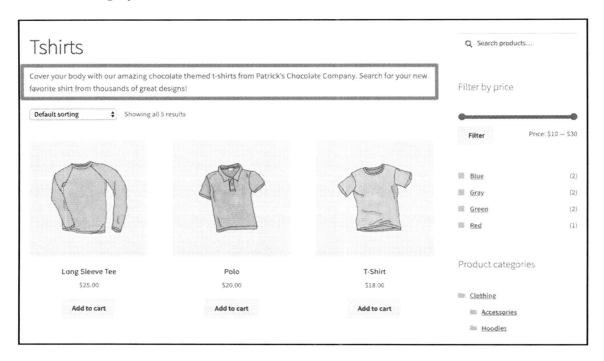

In the Storefront theme, you can see the description above the products. Different themes will display this in slightly different places but above the products is pretty common.

The Storefront doesn't display a product category thumbnail but some themes will. Even though not all themes will display the category thumbnail, this image is sometimes selected to be shared on social media, so you might want to select an image in case this page is shared on social media.

Let's see how to add proper context for the products in the following section.

Context matters

One thing your product category description can do is provide context. Let's say you're selling mice for laptops and computers. If you have a product category called **Mice** and you have products called **Red Mouse** and **Blue Mouse**, search engines won't know whether you're talking about:

- Mice—the animal
- Mice—the computer accessory

The category description can provide that context. If you're selling computer mice, make sure to mention that in your description.

Meta description for categories

In addition to writing a good description for the page itself, you can write a meta description that will catch someone's eye so they click on your page in the search engine results page.

To add a meta description to your product category, you'll have to install a **Search Engine Optimization (SEO)** plugin. I'll install the Yoast SEO plugin (`https://wordpress.org/plugins/wordpress-seo/`), which is available for free on `https://wordpress.org`:

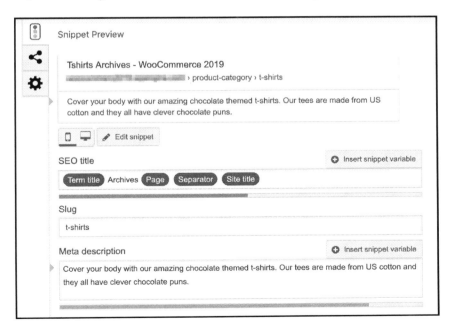

With this plugin, you can write a meta description that will be displayed on the **Search Engine Results Page (SERP)** and you'll see a preview within your admin. This is a good place to use alternate terms such as t-shirts, tees, and T-shirts.

Search engines bold any searched terms on the SERP, so if the user searched for `good looking tees`, then *tees* in my description will be bolded and will draw their eye.

You can also customize the SEO title. `Tshirts Archives` isn't that helpful. We can probably remove `Archives` so it's clear this is a list of t-shirts.

A pretty category description

Once you install Yoast SEO, you might have noticed that your product category description field is now a rich text field where you can bold, italicize, add images, add headings, and so on, as shown in the following screenshot:

The default category description used to be plaintext. Now it's rich text.

URLs

Something that's always important for SEO is to have clear URLs. You want to have one clear term in your product category page. So, you might want to have the following:

- t-shirt
- tshirt
- tee

But you definitely don't want this:

- t-shirt-tshirt-tee

Search engines will likely penalize you. So, make sure you pick the most popular option for your industry and use that. If you already installed an SEO plugin such as Yoast SEO, you can edit the **Slug** field:

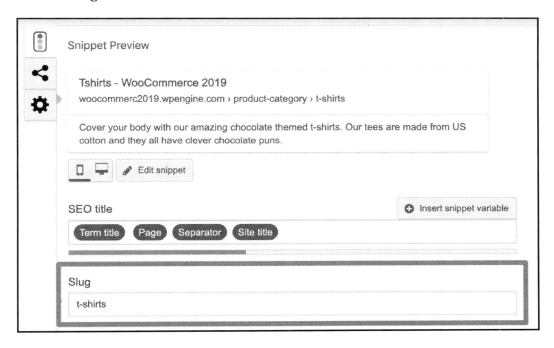

If you aren't using Yoast SEO, you can do this in WooCommerce itself under **Products | Categories | {{pick a category}} | Edit** and then edit the **Slug** field.

Redirects in WordPress

One thing you should know about is changing URLs. WordPress does a pretty good job logging all URLs and when one of the URLs is changed, it's saved in the database and a redirect is automatically created. So if you created a product category called **T-shirts** and you change it to **t-shirts**, the old URL should redirect to the new URL.

This is fantastic behavior *unless* an admin changes the URL back to the original URL. If you go from **tshirts** to **t-shirts** and then back to **tshirts** again, you might have an issue with infinite redirects.

Our product archive page is a lot easier to read and a lot easier for search engines to find. Now, we can look into improving the Shop page with product filters.

Adding product filters to your Shop page

Since we're organizing the products in your store, if you haven't installed and activated Storefront, now is a good time to do so. You'll want to have a sidebar so we can add widgets to help our users to filter products:

1. You can do this by going to **Appearance** | **Themes** | **Storefront** | **Activate**.

   When you do so, you'll see a nag to install a home page and a list of products. I'm going to do both so we have a lot of products to sort through:

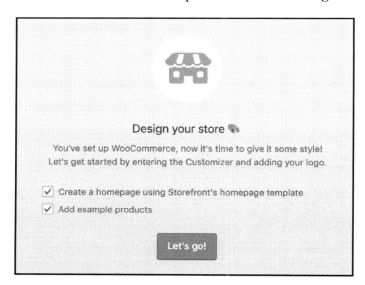

2. Once you do and you click **Let's go!**, you'll be taken to the WordPress customizer:

If you aren't automatically taken here, you can get to the customizer through **Appearance | Customize** in your admin.

Let's customize our Shop page. To do that, follow the steps given here:

1. Click on **Shop** from within the customizer, which will load the page:

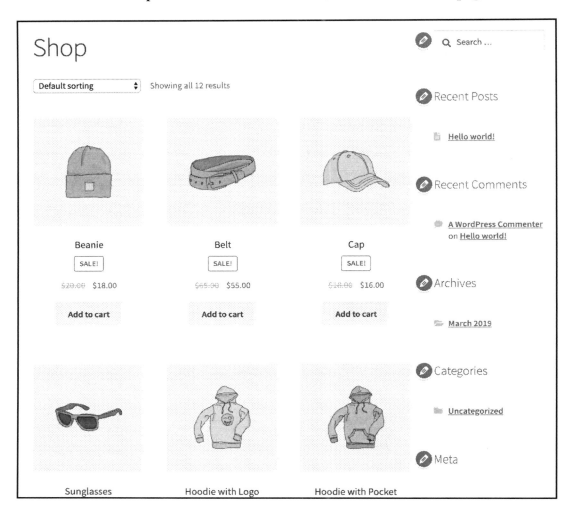

By default, down the right-hand side, we see the following:

- **Search**
- **Recent Posts**
- **Recent Comments**
- **Archives**
- **Categories**
- **Meta**

And for some blogs, these are fine. But for an online store, we want to be able to search and filter products.

2. In the sidebar of the customizer, click **Widgets | Sidebar** and you'll see the list of widgets:

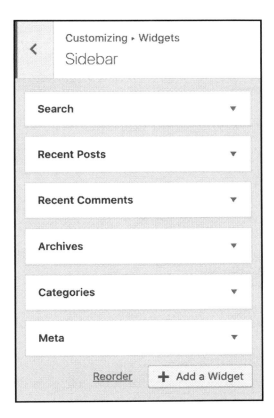

3. Go ahead and open these by clicking the drop-down arrow. Click **Remove** to delete the widget. Delete all of the widgets.

4. Then, it's time to add useful widgets to our store. Click **Add a Widget** and type in woocommerce to see a list of widgets designed for WooCommerce:

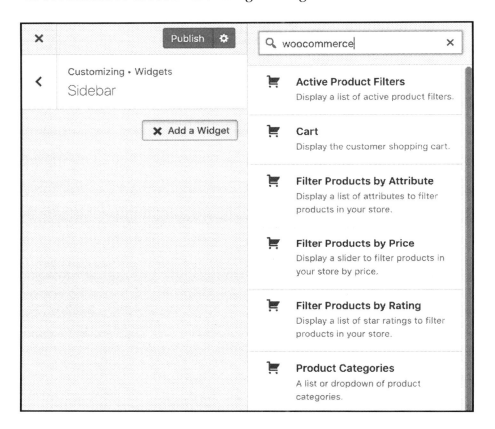

5. Add the following widgets:

   - **Product Search**
   - **Active Product Filters**
   - **Filter Products by Attribute**
   - **Filter Products by Price**
   - **Filter Products by Rating**
   - **Product Categories**
   - **Recent Product Reviews**

The following widgets can be seen in the following image:

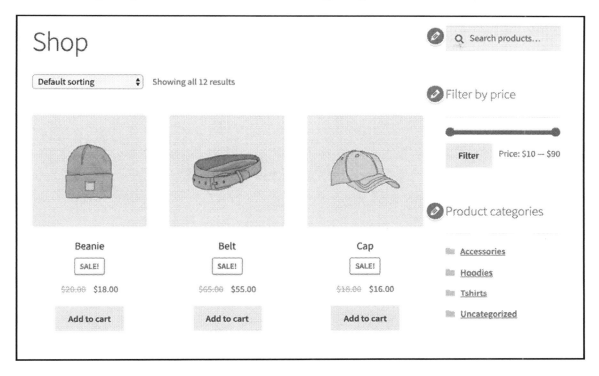

Now, let's get started with hidden widgets in the following section.

Hidden widgets

You might notice that not every widget shows up. For example, where are the product attributes?

Widgets in WordPress are pretty smart and they only show up if they're relevant. If none of your products have attributes, then you won't see the attribute filtering widget. The same thing happens with product reviews: if there are no recent reviews, then there's nothing to display.

Let's add some product attributes, such as color, to our store. You can read `Chapter 2, Configuring Products`, to see how to add global product attributes. Once you do, you can see them in the sidebar and then you can click them and start filtering the products.

Once you have a global product attribute, you can customize your **Filter Products by Attribute** widget:

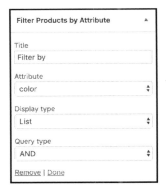

You need to select one attribute. In our case, that's going to be color. But if you have multiple attributes such as color, size, and cut, you can add multiple **Filter Products by Attribute** widgets.

Active product filters

I've gone ahead and clicked on a color (**Red**) and set a maximum price range. Now, with the active product filter, we see the exact parameters we set on our products:

Product filters are somewhat useful for a dozen products but as you get into hundreds or thousands of products, product filters let your users browse according to their needs.

The Active Product Filters widget lets users see those parameters and remove them. You don't technically need this widget but without it, some users will be confused about how to remove parameters.

Filters make your Shop page much easier to navigate and I strongly recommend them. Once you've made the Shop page easy to navigate, we can look into adding product blocks around our site.

Understanding Product blocks

With WordPress 5.0 (Gutenberg) came blocks and the WooCommerce team immediately started creating custom blocks for products (`https://woocommerce.com/posts/making-it-easier-to-add-products-to-posts-and-pages-with-the-products-block-for-gutenberg/`).

To see how powerful these blocks are, go to the admin page, then go to **Pages** | **Homepage** and see how the home page was created. We can see a list of all of the available blocks here:

- **Products by Category block**
- **Newest Products block**
- **Hand-picked Products block**
- **Top Rated Products block**
- **On Sale Products block**
- **Best Selling Products block**

All of the features are built with the new blocks. If you want to see all of the blocks included in WooCommerce, add a new block to any WordPress post and type in woocommerce:

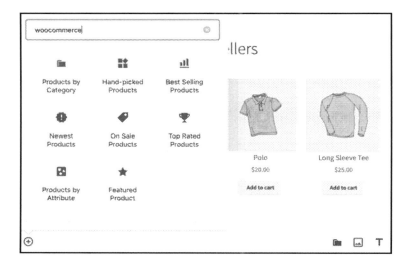

A list of product blocks for WooCommerce is shown that can be added to any page including the home page.

Let's look into creating our own product page.

Single product pages

With this much control, it's really easy to create great home pages. But you can also create fantastic single product pages or product release posts. Let's create a brand new post and talk about the new product we just released.

Go to **Posts** | **Add new** in your admin page and use a combination of these blocks to make a release post:

- Cover image
- Image
- Paragraph
- Hand-picked products

Here's what I came up within just 5 minutes, grabbing free images from Unsplash (https://unsplash.com):

Smiles for Everyone

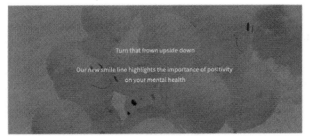

Turn that frown upside down

Our new smile line highlights the importance of positivity
on your mental health

Lorem ipsum dolor sit amet, consectetur adipiscing elit, sed do eiusmod tempor incididunt ut labore et dolore magna aliqua. Dignissim diam quis enim lobortis. A arcu cursus vitae congue. Tellus orci ac auctor augue mauris augue neque.

Tellus in metus vulputate eu scelerisque felis imperdiet proin fermentum. Condimentum lacinia quis vel eros donec ac odio tempor orci. Pulvinar pellentesque habitant morbi tristique senectus et netus et.

Lorem ipsum dolor sit amet consectetur adipiscing. Non tellus orci ac auctor augue mauris. Leo urna molestie at elementum eu facilisis sed odio morbi. Eget velit aliquet sagittis id consectetur.

Nibh sed pulvinar proin gravida hendrerit lectus. Nibh praesent tristique magna sit. Convallis convallis tellus id interdum. Mauris cursus mattis molestie a iaculis at. Tempor nec feugiat nisl pretium fusce. Felis imperdiet proin fermentum leo vel orci porta. Ipsum a arcu cursus vitae congue mauris rhoncus. Enim sit amet venenatis urna cursus eget nunc.

Hoodie with Logo
$45.00

Add to cart

Curabitur vitae nunc sed velit dignissim sodales. Mi quis hendrerit dolor magna eget. Et netus et malesuada fames ac turpis egestas. Nisl purus in mollis nunc sed. Purus ut faucibus pulvinar elementum integer enim neque volutpat ac.

Mauris commodo quis imperdiet massa tincidunt nunc pulvinar sapien. Purus viverra accumsan in nisl nisi scelerisque eu ultrices vitae. Sed nisl lacus sed viverra. Leo urna molestie at elementum eu facilisis. Sed viverra ipsum nunc aliquet. Id semper risus in hendrerit. Quis imperdiet massa tincidunt nunc pulvinar sapien et. Praesent tristique magna sit amet.

A iaculis at erat pellentesque adipiscing commodo elit. Augue interdum velit euismod in pellentesque massa placerat duis ultricies. Sit amet risus nullam eget felis. Venenatis cras sed felis eget velit aliquet. Quis varius quam quisque id diam vel. Tempor nec feugiat nisl pretium fusce. Felis imperdiet proin fermentum leo vel orci porta. Ipsum a arcu cursus vitae congue mauris rhoncus. Enim sit amet venenatis urna cursus eget nunc. Sodales ut eu sem integer vitae justo eget magna. Ut lectus arcu bibendum at varius vel pharetra vel. Sed arcu non odio euismod lacinia at quis risus sed. Id donec ultrices tincidunt arcu non sodales.

You can, of course, do a lot better with more than 5 minutes. I only used one WooCommerce-related block on the page, but you can use many blocks. These don't have to be regular web pages—they can be announcement posts or anywhere you see the modern Gutenberg block editor in your admin.

Customizing product blocks

When you add a product block to your post, there are several settings you'll want to tweak:

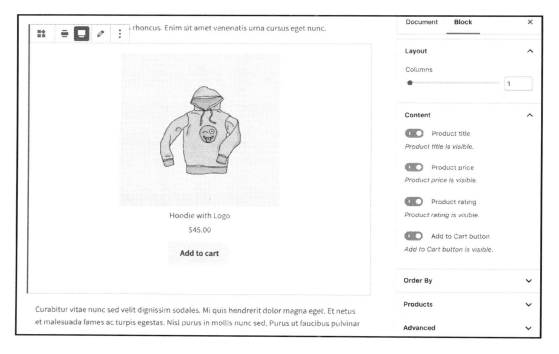

The first is likely to be the **Columns**. If you're highlighting a set of new products, make sure you have the right number of columns for your products. I'm only showing one new product so one column will work fine.

Note: I'm choosing to show all product information (title, price, ratings, and the **Add to cart** button) but WooCommerce is smart and leaves the rating empty until there are ratings. Once a user rates this product, this will dynamically appear.

If you need to change the products on display, you can click into **Products** under **Block Settings** and add, edit, or remove products.

Featuring a product

The best way to feature a product is with the **Hand-Picked Products** block but I expect this to change (maybe even by the time this book comes out). There will likely be a featured product released at some point that displays a much larger product image, short description, price, and **Add to cart** button.

Keep an eye on the product blocks as they're a fantastic way to make use of all of the content power built into WordPress.

And keep an eye on blocks: in general, if you go onto WordPress.org, you'll see blocks for many features, such as testimonials, graphs, and graphics.

The value of blocks

What's so great about these new blocks is they show you what your user will see on the frontend and they display dynamic content. That means if you ever update your featured image, price, or even the title of the product, all of that will be changed wherever you use these blocks.

With some of my clients, they don't want to mention product details such as the price in a release post because the price might change and they don't want users to be confused. With blocks, you don't have to worry about that at all. It's dynamic content visually displayed in the post editor, which is perfect for store owners.

Summary

We looked at all of the ways to organize your products so users can easily find them and search engines can send you more traffic. From very basic techniques such as adding categories and tags to more advanced techniques such as adding product filters and using product blocks in the Gutenberg editor, you have a variety of tools to help users to find the right product for them.

Organizing products is a bit of art and science. It's worth doing some research before you launch your store to take your best guess at the organization. But once you start getting real-life users, you can analyze their browsing and search habits to see whether you can make improvements.

Now, we can learn how to optimize the rest of our site for search engines (called SEO) and learn how to attract traffic in the next chapter.

Optimizing SEO and Attracting Traffic

You can have the perfect e-commerce site with thousands of products, perfect organization and searching, easy-to-use payment options and cheap shipping. Unfortunately, none of that will do you any good unless you can get people to your website.

Bringing people to a regular website is called traffic generation. In the e-commerce world, you're trying to bring people to your site to make purchases. This is called customer acquisition, and **customer acquisition cost (CAC)** is one of the main indicators of a successful e-commerce business. If you can reliably bring traffic to your site, a small percentage of that traffic will purchase products, and you'll make money.

There are techniques to build a strong e-commerce business, like securing recurring purchases, increasing conversion rates, and lowering your product costs, but none of them matter without the initial traffic! One of the main techniques to bring in traffic is **search engine optimization (SEO)**—basically, getting search engines to recommend your site more often. So if there's one thing you should focus on after you build your store, it's customer acquisition.

We're going to look into the following topics:

- Optimizing your presence on search engines
- Keyword research for search engine optimization and search engine marketing
- Creating a sitemap to help the organization
- Configuring breadcrumbs
- Creating and sharing an XML sitemap

First up is optimizing your presence on search engines.

Optimizing your search engine presence (SEO)

There are many ways to bring people to your site. The following are some of the best methods:

- Paid advertising
- Social Media
- Influencer marketing
- Affiliate programs
- Trade shows
- Business development
- Speaking engagements
- Public relations
- Content marketing
- Search engine optimization (SEO)

We don't have time to go into every single strategy. We'd need several books to do so. But we do have time to talk about how SEO and content marketing (a related strategy) are different from the rest.

Let's first look at some of the most talked-about strategies, which are usually advert-related and cost money to get up and running. Then we'll look at the slow but steady increase in visitors from SEO.

Transactional marketing strategies

Most customer acquisition strategies are transactional. By that, I mean you do something once and you get a certain number of visitors, for example:

- You spend $10 on a Facebook advert and get 300 visitors.
- You go to a trade show and meet 100 people who eventually become customers.
- You announce a new product that gets picked up by the media and you get 1,000 visitors to your store.
- You send out a funny video on Twitter and you get 100 visitors.

Most of these require ongoing effort or money for them to bring in visitors. However, search engine optimization and its cousin content marketing are different. You take the time to optimize your site or write an article once and they continually bring in visitors.

Acquiring free traffic

If you write a high-quality article so search engines think you're the best result for a particular query, it can bring in dozens all the way up to thousands of visitors a month.

I've been writing about e-commerce for years on my blog. The posts that I wrote 8 years ago are still bringing in traffic every month.

However, this process takes some time. For search engines to recognize that your site provides value, both your site and the post have to be around for a while. Search engines also rely on other sites linking to you, and of course, it takes a while to write the articles.

Let's say you can write one article a week and those articles generate only 20 visitors a month for the first several months. That's a lot of effort for a total of 80 visitors. And with a typical 1% conversion rate that's 0.8 orders.

SEO and content marketing can be great but they have a very slow ramp-up time, so you'll want to combine them with other strategies that bring in a huge number of visitors for a one-off cost.

Let's investigate which keywords are most popular in helping with both SEO and advert-buying strategies.

Researching keywords for e-commerce

Before you optimize your site, it's worth doing the research to know what you should optimize for. Doing keyword research helps you figure out which words or phrases people are searching for and which ones you can actually rank for.

Most stores open without doing any research, and they think they'll rank for hugely popular terms such as the following:

- Shoes
- T-shirts
- Chocolate
- Razor subscription

These terms are *highly* competitive. With a little research, using tools later in this section, you can optimize your site for search terms that are much easier to rank for. We'll look into the following:

- Creating a list of potential keywords
- Comparing the search volume of different keywords
- Optimizing for the best solution

Once you know how to do all of these, you'll know which terms you can try to rank for in search engines to get some free traffic.

Creating a list of keywords

The first step to optimizing your site for search engines is to create a list of long-tail keywords. Long-tail keywords are multiple words combined together, for example:

- Canvas shoes
- Nerdy t-shirts
- Healthy chocolate
- Men's razor subscription

These are going to be much easier to rank for, and the more words you can come up with the easier it will be to find a keyword you can try to optimize.

Let's take an actual example from a local WooCommerce store, The Chocolate Therapist (`https://www.thechocolatetherapist.com`). They sell chocolate and talk about the health benefits (when eaten in moderation!).

Some keywords they might come up with include the following:

- Chocolate
- Dark chocolate
- Healthy chocolate
- Health benefits of chocolate
- Small batch chocolate
- Gluten-free chocolate
- Dairy-free chocolate
- Soy-free chocolate
- Dairy chocolate
- Chocolate and wine pairing

And you could go on and on and come up with lists of hundreds or even thousands of keywords.

Comparing search volume

Once you have your list, it's time to figure out which terms are the most popular. There are tons of tools that compare search volume on search engines. Some of the more popular tools are the following:

- SEMrush
- KWFinder
- SpyFu

Many of these tools are paid. But you can get an idea of search volume using Google Trends. You can type in multiple phrases and compare search volume. It won't tell you about the exact searches, as you'll need a paid tool for that, but you can get an idea of how popular certain terms are.

Here's my comparison of **healthy chocolate** versus **health benefits of chocolate**:

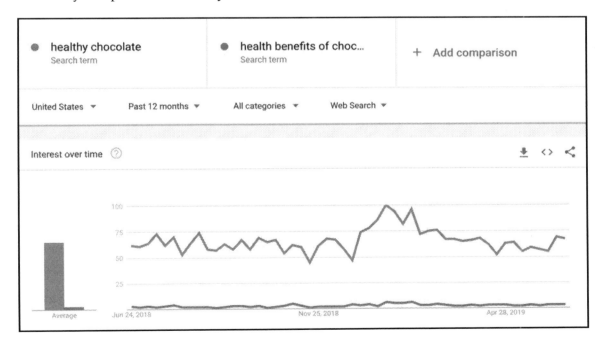

You can see that **healthy chocolate** is much more popular than **health benefits of chocolate**. Now I know that I should use that phrase throughout my site and minimize using **health benefits of chocolate**. Google Trends shows you a small number of keywords. Some of the paid tools let you upload a CSV file to compare hundreds or thousands of keywords.

Let's see how to optimize the searching for keywords in the next section.

Optimizing for keywords

Once you know which words are most popular and which keywords have the least competition, you can use that terminology throughout the site. You can use it in your product descriptions, blog posts, URLs, downloads, tag lines, page titles, and so on.

As an example, I might do research and find that *two-player games* are more popular than *games for couples*. I should then weave *two-player games* into the body section, into blog posts, into image alt tags, and maybe even into product titles and I should try to avoid using *games for couples*.

You don't want to spam your site. It should always sound natural if you read it out loud, but instead of using whatever sounds good at the time, you want to use a keyword so search engines know what your site is about and will show it on the **Search Engines Results Page** (**SERP**).

There are entire books written about SEO, but this is a quick overview that should help you in getting started with optimizing your site for search engines. As with most marketing strategies, there's always more you can do, but this should help you appear in search engines and get your first free visitors.

Next up is a strategy we can use to help us make sure we organize our site to bring in the traffic from search engines.

Creating a sitemap

One of the things you can do before you create your site is to create a sitemap. A sitemap will make sure your site is structured properly so you can optimize for keywords, and make it obvious to users how to navigate your store. Having the proper structure can really help search engines understand what's on your site and whether they should send users to your site.

Making a sitemap usually only takes an hour or two, and if you're building a site for a client, it can clear up a huge amount of uncertainty for both of you.

The following diagram shows a sitemap:

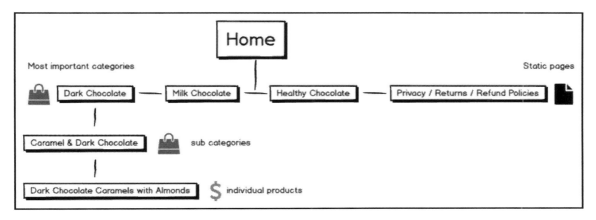

I like to start by adding the home page at the top, then add the top-level (most important) categories and static pages, then add subcategories and, finally, list out individual products.

This is a visual guide as to what the site will look like. I use a tool called Balsamiq (https://balsamiq.com), but any tool will do, even Microsoft Word, to create simple sitemaps.

The benefit of creating sitemaps before we start coding our site is that we can clearly see if important content is missing. For example, if you sell clothing, you might want a page on sizing, showing your clothing on different sized models.

By making sure we are covering all of the required content for our site, we have a lot of pages where visitors from search engines can land. And by having a clear structure, search engines will be more likely to send visitors to the right page. When users don't hit the back button and immediately continue searching, the search engines assume the user found what they wanted so they should have a good idea of how many people are landing on the right page.

With our list of pages and categories, we can now look into optimizing our breadcrumbs.

Configuring breadcrumbs

Let's say a visitor lands on the caramel and dark chocolate product category. They might like what they see, but they might want to look at dark chocolate without caramel.

If you build your site poorly, the user will have to go all the way back to the Shop or home page and then navigate to the parent category.

By default, WooCommerce will add breadcrumbs to your product and category pages. Breadcrumbs show your users how to navigate back to the home or Shop page.

In this example, we see the breadcrumbs **Home** | **Tshirts** | **Vneck Tshirt**. In Storefront, a product page will look something like this:

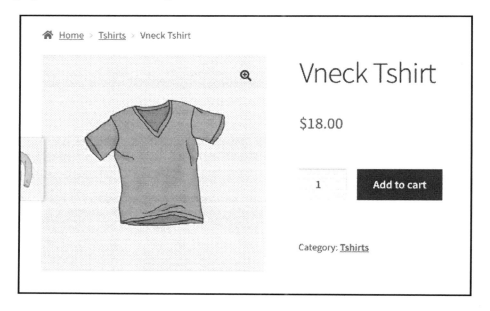

And a category page will look something like this:

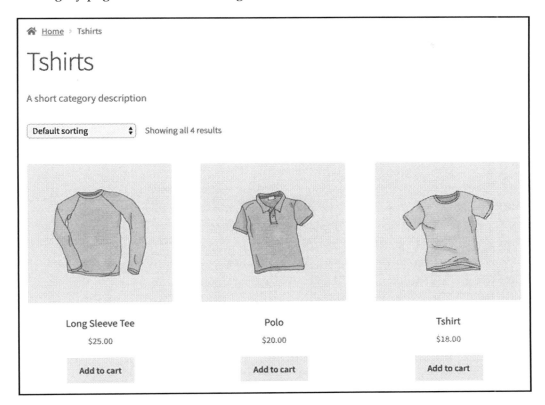

This is controlled entirely by WooCommerce. But it can be modified by your theme. By default, any theme should have breadcrumbs on the product and category pages. But if your theme does something atypical, you might not see them.

If you want to add or customize breadcrumbs, the best way is to add a custom **Personal Home Page** (**PHP**) code to your theme.

Adding custom PHP code

If you're familiar with customizing themes, you can add a little bit of code to your theme and breadcrumbs will automatically be added.

Add the following code to a theme template and you're good to go:

```php
<?php woocommerce_breadcrumb(); ?>
```

Or, if you want to customize the functionality, there are a few parameters you can adjust. You can pass in a $args array and in that array you can modify the following fields:

- delimiter: The character to display between the breadcrumbs
- wrap_before: The breadcrumbs container starting code
- wrap_after: The breadcrumbs container ending code
- before: HTML to display before the breadcrumbs
- after: HTML to display after the breadcrumbs
- home: Include the front page at the beginning of the breadcrumbs

Here's an example where I customized the delimiter (what is displayed between the links), and I manually added text before the breadcrumbs render:

```php
<?php
        $args = array(
                'delimiter' => '/',
                'before' => '<span class="breadcrumb-title">' . __(
                'This is where you are:',
                'woothemes' ) . '</span>'
        );
?>
<?php woocommerce_breadcrumb( $args ); ?>
```

If you want to customize the breadcrumb, you can refer to the official documentation (https://docs.woocommerce.com/document/woocommerce_breadcrumb/).

Using a plugin

Using plugins is another way to add breadcrumbs to your site. These plugins could just affect WooCommerce or they could apply to your whole site. One of the more popular plugins is Breadcrumb NavXT (`https://wordpress.org/plugins/breadcrumb-navxt/`):

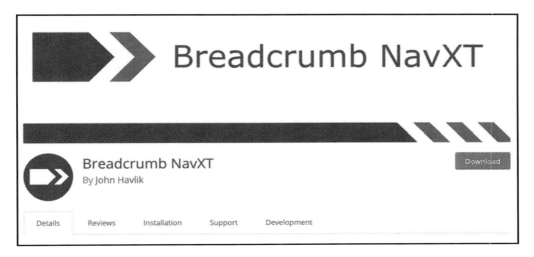

Here's the plugin on WordPress `https://wordpress.org`. They're easy to use, and if they do what you need, they're generally a better solution than coding your own solution.

Another tool we can use is a plugin to generate and share XML sitemaps.

Adding XML sitemaps

An important tool to help search robots like Google understand the structure of your site is an XML sitemap. An XML sitemap lists a website's important pages, making sure Google and other search engines can find and crawl them all, and helps them to understand your website structure.

Here are the first few listings on the sitemap I use on my personal site:

You can see I have 296 URLs on my site and the sitemaps list them all and make it easy for search engines to understand when they were published, which category they're in, and where they're located.

Let's set this up with Yoast SEO.

Adding an XML sitemap with Yoast SEO

As you can see, my sitemap is created through the `Yoast SEO` plugin. There are other XML sitemap plugins out there, but since you're likely using Yoast SEO for other search engine optimization uses, you might as well use this functionality so you don't have to install a new plugin.

1. Go ahead and install the plugin if you haven't yet.
2. Then in the WordPress admin click **Yoast SEO | General**.
3. And then click the **Features** tab.

From here, you'll see a list of features that are included in Yoast, as shown in the following screenshot:

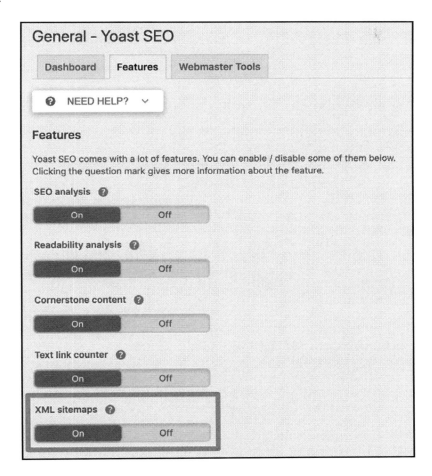

Once you verify your XML sitemap is enabled, you can click the little **?** icon. From here, you can click **See the XML sitemap** to view your sitemap. You'll want to make sure it's publicly viewable before the next step:

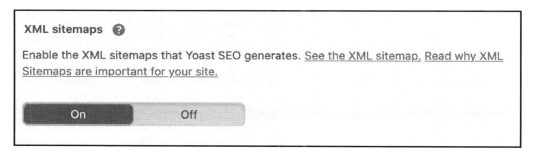

If you're reading this book months from now, the functionality for XML sitemaps might change. You might not be able to use plugins like Yoast and instead have to do it through WordPress itself.

Possible movement of XML sitemaps to WordPress Core

There's an official proposal to add XML sitemaps to WordPress core so you wouldn't need an SEO plugin such as Yoast to add this functionality to your site (`https://make.wordpress.org/core/2019/06/12/xml-sitemaps-feature-project-proposal/`).

If this happens, the XML sitemap's functionality in Yoast SEO will likely be removed and instead, you'll find it in the WordPress **Admin** under either **Settings** or **Tools**.

Let's see how to submit an XML sitemap on Google in the next section.

Submitting an XML sitemap to Google

It's possible for search engines to find your XML sitemap without you having to do anything. However, to make sure the XML sitemap is utilized fully, you should submit it to Google Search Console (formerly Google Webmaster Tools: `https://search.google.com/search-console`). Follow these steps:

1. Head over to **Google Search Console,** and create a new site.
2. Once you've created your site in **Google Search Console,** you'll see a link for **Sitemaps**.

   Here's what **Google Search Console** looks like for my site:

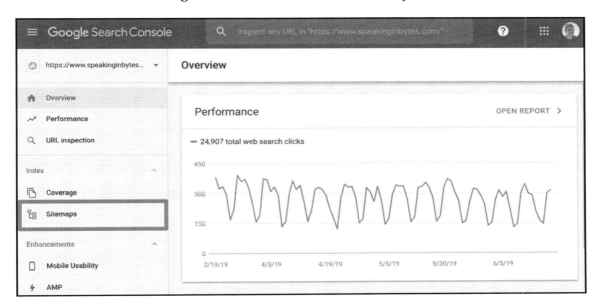

3. From here, you just type in the URL of your sitemap that's generated by Yoast SEO. Typically, it's `sitemap_index.xml`:

4. Once you submit it, you should see it listed on that page. After a little time for scanning, Google should show you how many links it discovered:

| /sitemap.xml | Sitemap index | Dec 16, 2016 | Jun 13, 2019 | Success | 445 | |

If you're intentional with the keywords you use on your site, you plan your site with a sitemap, you have breadcrumbs, and an XML sitemap, you should be well on your way to having a website optimized for SEO.

Summary

In this chapter, we learned why SEO is so important, including how to find the right keywords and why you need to create a sitemap. We also learned how to configure breadcrumbs, and finally how to create and submit an XML sitemap for your sitemap.

Having optimized many parts of the store, we should see an increase in organic traffic from search engines like Google. That will definitely help the store stay in business and, hopefully, make a ton of money so we can keep developing functionality for the store.

In the next chapter, we will learn how to manage sales in WooCommerce.

Managing Sales Through WP Admin 5

There's a lot of attention placed on creating products for your store. But despite how important adding products is, it doesn't actually take up that much time. Once your store is up and running, you'll spend a lot more time managing orders. This chapter will cover the following topics, which are just a few of the responsibilities that store owners have to handle:

- Fulfilling orders
- Refunding orders and payments
- Viewing internal sales data
- Viewing third-party sales data

Once you know how to do all of these things, you should be able to manage your own online store.

Fulfilling orders

When people take out their credit card to pay for things with their hard-earned cash, they expect you to ship their order quickly and safely. Getting a package from your warehouse to a customer's home is called fulfillment, and there are a bunch of smaller steps included. They are as follows:

- New order notification
- Viewing customer shipping information
- Packing items into boxes
- Printing shipping labels
- Dropping off packages
- Marking orders as completed

Exploring new order notifications

The whole process starts with a notification, which WooCommerce has automatically enabled. You can view the notification email under **WooCommerce** | **Settings** | **Emails**, as shown in the following image:

By default, these emails will be sent to the site admin. You can click **Manage** to change the recipient, or to add extra recipients.

New orders badge in the site admin

If you're browsing through the WordPress admin panel, you can also see orders on the menu. Click on **WooCommerce** in the **Admin** menu, and you can see the number of new orders.

It will look like the following image:

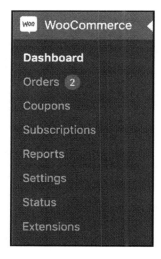

This shows the number of new orders. If you view the orders but you don't fulfill them, this notification bubble will disappear.

Browsing orders

If you want to see all of your orders, you can browse through them by clicking on **WooCommerce** | **Orders** from within the WordPress admin, as shown in the following image:

You can very easily see which orders are **Processing**. Processing means an order has been paid for, but not yet shipped. Once you ship the order, you should change the status to **Completed**.

Either way, once you know that there's a new order, you now need to know what items need to be packed and where to send those items.

Viewing shipping information

On the **Orders** page in WooCommerce, you can click on the little eye icon next to the order as shown in the previous image. It will show you a little preview with the shipping details and a list of the items that need packing.

The details will resemble the ones in the following image:

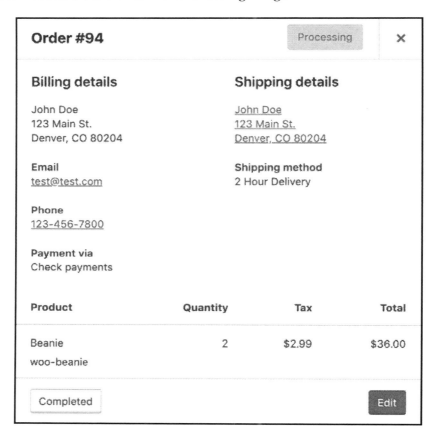

You could pack all of the items at the bottom of this screen, drop the package off at a shipper (courier service), and mark the order as complete by clicking **Completed**.

On the **Orders** page, you could also click on the **Order number | customer name** to see the **Edit order** screen with a lot more detail, as shown here:

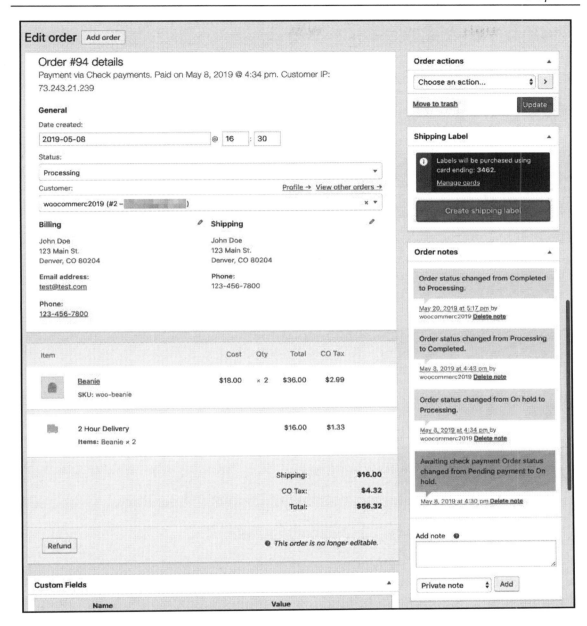

Here, we can again see shipping information, communicate with the customer, edit any information, print shipping labels, or start a refund. It's a little slower to load a whole new page rather than using the preview functionality, but you get a lot more options on this page.

Packing the boxes

If you're just getting started, you might be confused about which boxes you should use. And unfortunately, the software doesn't help you at all. Live shipping rates such as UPS, USPS, and FedEx have a box packer built-in (`https://docs.woocommerce.com/document/understanding-box-packing-calculations/`), which is how you can get accurate estimates on shipping costs.

Unfortunately, there's no way to access this box packer in the admin. But you can choose which boxes your box packer can use. If you're just getting started, you can save yourself a lot of time by having a small set of boxes that you use.

You can go to **WooCommerce** | **Settings** | **Shipping** | **WooCommerce Services**. At the bottom, you can click **Add package**, as shown in the following image:

 You have to have installed WooCommerce Services in order to see this menu option. If you have installed other shipping extensions, you might have to find similar settings under a different menu.

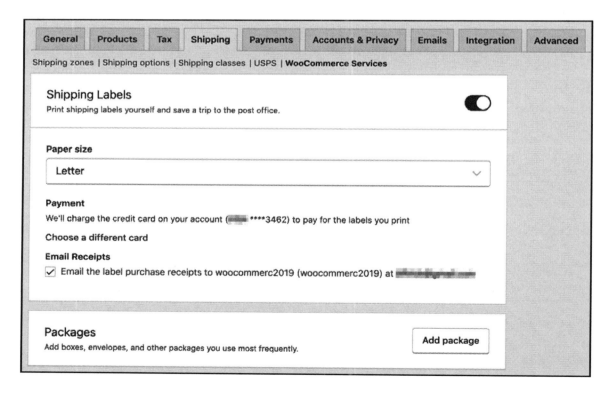

You can select pre-created boxes on the **Service package** tab, as shown here:

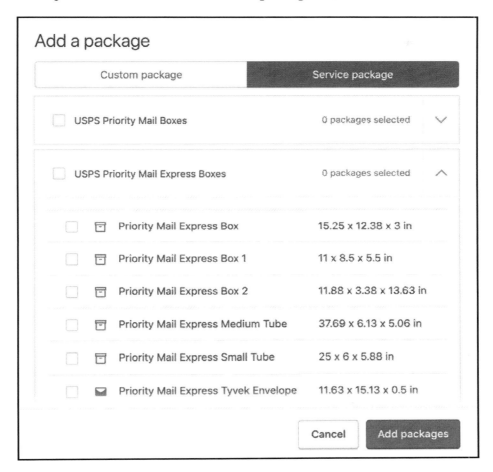

You can also create brand new packages under **Custom package**. For most stores, you won't need to know how to do that. But sometimes, you can save a lot of money if you tend to ship unique package sizes.

A good example of this is a sunglasses store, with which I have had a recent experience. They often sell one pair of sunglasses at a time, so they ship them in a very small, tight box, in order to protect the sunglasses and save them shipping costs.

Printing shipping labels

Once you have your boxes ready to go, you can print out shipping labels. Using the **Edit order** screen, you have the opportunity to print out a shipping label, as seen here:

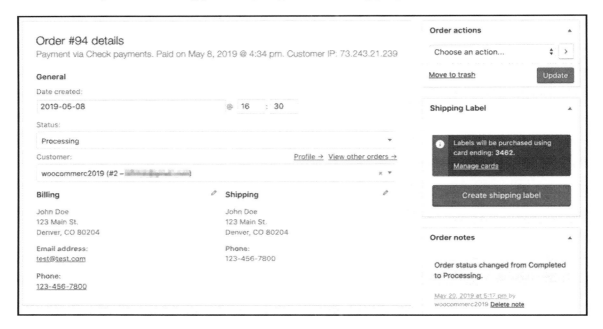

 This is powered by WooCommerce Services, so you have to have this plugin installed and activated to see this button.

You'll be asked to confirm your **Origin address** and the **Destination address**. Then, you can select packages and add a weight (if necessary), as shown here:

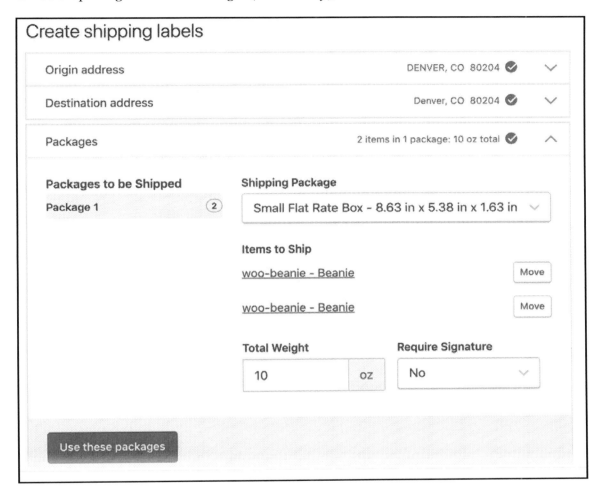

Click **Use these packages**, and then you can select your rate, as shown in the following image:

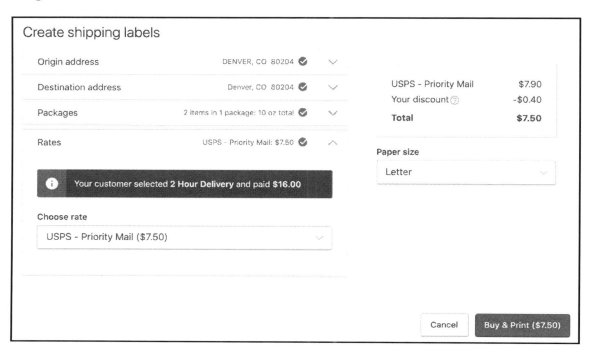

Finally, you can select **Buy & Print**. You'll get a PDF file, and you can print it out on your printer at home.

If you happen to have a label printer, you can change the **Paper size** field, and select a smaller size that will work with a label printer.

Dropping off packages

Once your packages are packed and have shipping labels attached, you're ready to drop them off. You can, of course, manually go into your shipping provider's office and drop off the packages.

But once you start getting more than a couple of orders a week, you'll want to schedule pickups. Most shipping providers will let you schedule pickups ahead of time, and you can even have a recurring pickup time.

If you're in the US, you can use **United States Postal Service (USPS)**, which has a very easy to tool to schedule a pickup. I won't get into detail here, but I've documented this process on my site (`https://www.speakinginbytes.com/2017/11/schedule-usps-pickup/`).

Marking orders as completed

Whether you print out labels, or manually drop packages off in your own car, the last step is to mark an order as completed.

You can change the status of the order to **Complete** on the **Edit orders** page, as seen here:

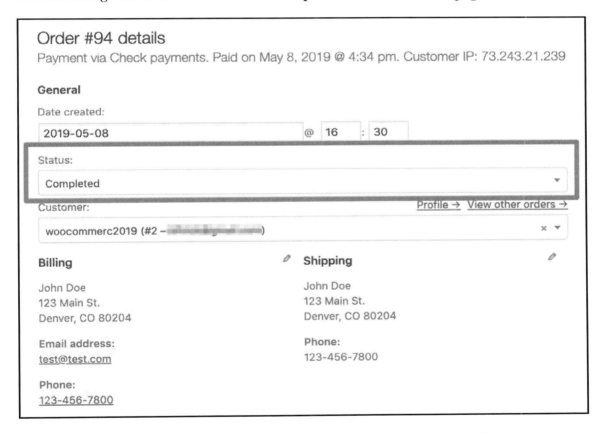

Once you have marked an order as being complete, you're done. You can ship the rest of the orders and then move onto another task. Now, let's learn how to reimburse the users in the next section.

Refunding orders and payments

Of course, no matter how well you provide your services, such as advertising, describing, and shipping the products, some users will be unhappy and will want a refund. Refund rates vary wildly from industry to industry. Some industries will have refund rates in the low single digits, for example, 1-3%, whereas other industries, such as fashion, can have refund rates up to 25-30%, which is massive.

Once you've had a few refund requests, you'll want to build a process to make it easier. Let's start with manual refunds, and then look into building a refund process.

Refund requests

If a customer emails you, tweets you, or calls you for a refund, you'll have to know how to make a refund. This can be done on the **Edit order** page.

The following image shows the functionality:

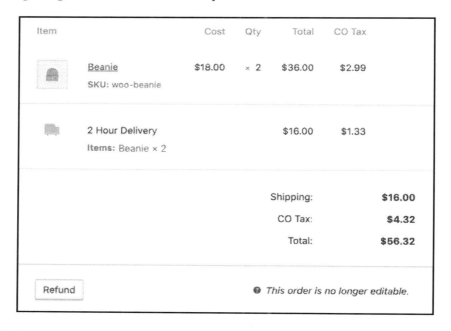

You can click the **Refund** button, which changes the **Qty** field to an input field, where you can choose how many items you want to refund. In our case, let's say someone wants to keep only one hat, and they want to return the other one.

You can manually type in the reason (so it's logged) in the text box, as shown in the following image:

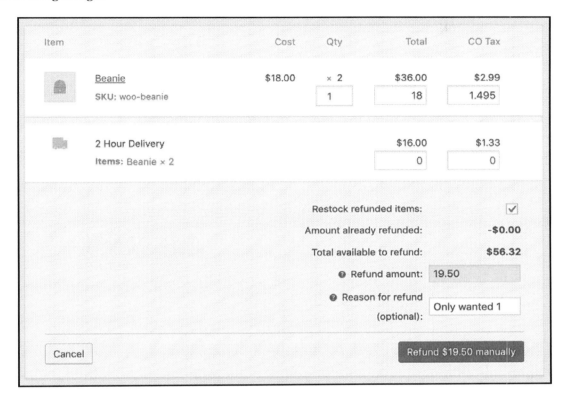

Then, depending on the payment gateway that you used to pay for the order, you'll see two buttons to refund. We only see one because we used a payment gateway that doesn't support automated refunds (in this case, Payment via Check, which is built into WooCommerce).

If you see the button on our screen that says **Refund $XX manually**, the order will be refunded in WooCommerce, but you still have to manually go into a payment gateway and refund their money in that system.

Some payment gateways, such as Stripe, support automatic refunds, and you'll see a **Refund $XX automatically** button. If you click that then the order will be refunded in WooCommerce, and it will also be refunded through Stripe.

If your payment gateway supports automatic refunds, you will almost always want to use that functionality so that you don't forget to manually refund in another system.

Building a refund request process

There are a number of ways to build a refund request process. For example, some third-party shipping companies, for example, Shippo (`https://goshippo.com/products/post-purchase-tracking/`), have a refund request process built in. That lets customers request refunds, print out shipping labels, and send them in. They built this in a self-serve manner so that the customer can do all of this, and you only pay for shipping labels when they're actually sent.

But, let's say that you want to keep this in WooCommerce. You can use WooCommerce Smart Refunder (`https://woocommerce.com/products/woocommerce-smart-refunder/`), which builds a refund request button onto the automatically generated **My Account** page:

And then, customers can fill out a form to request a refund, as shown here:

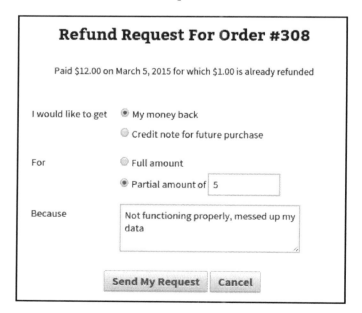

The admin can build rules to manually or automatically refund certain types of orders. And from the page where you moderate refund requests, if you approve the requests, they'll automatically refund the money and change the order status.

Having a process to refund orders is very useful, but it doesn't need to be done when you launch your store. You can wait until you get a few refunds to see what you want your process to look like.

You should now have a system to refund any orders that come in, which is an essential feature for an online store. Now that you can fulfill and refund orders, you can dig into the order data.

Viewing sales data

Once you've shipped your orders, you'll probably want to see which products and categories that the customers are interested in. When you have this data, you can buy more of the most profitable and the fastest-moving products. And, luckily for us, WooCommerce recently improved this experience quite a bit!

By the time you're reading this book, WooCommerce Admin (`https://wordpress.org/plugins/woocommerce-admin/`) should be have merged into WooCommerce and will be automatically included. But, at the time of writing, this is a beta plugin and the functionality is still changing. I'm going to show you what it looks like today, and it might change a little between now and when this book is published.

We're going to look into some basic data, which you can see at a glance on the **Orders** screen, as well as all of the data that you can dig into through the WooCommerce reports.

Admin banner

The new WooCommerce admin adds a banner across the top of most of the WooCommerce admin pages, which you can see here:

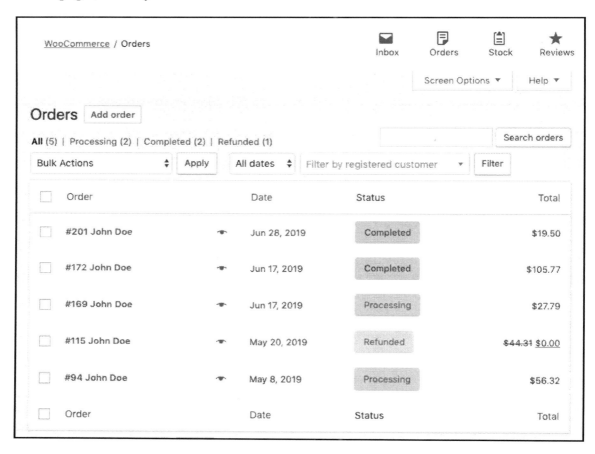

You can see where you are in the navigation, and you can click into **Inbox**, **Orders**, **Stock**, or **Reviews** to get more information.

From the **Orders** tab, you can see new orders, enabling you to see the latest handful of orders. But, more often than not, you'll want to see months or even years worth of data.

WooCommerce Analytics

If you click on **Analytics** in the admin menu you'll see a ton of reports, which are generated by the new WooCommerce admin. There are several reports available to you. They are as follows:

- Revenue
- Orders
- Products
- Categories
- Coupons
- Taxes
- Downloads
- Stock
- Customers

Out of all of these, Revenue, Products, Categories, Taxes, and Customers are my favorites. Let's take a look at the Revenue report to really dig in. It is shown in the following image:

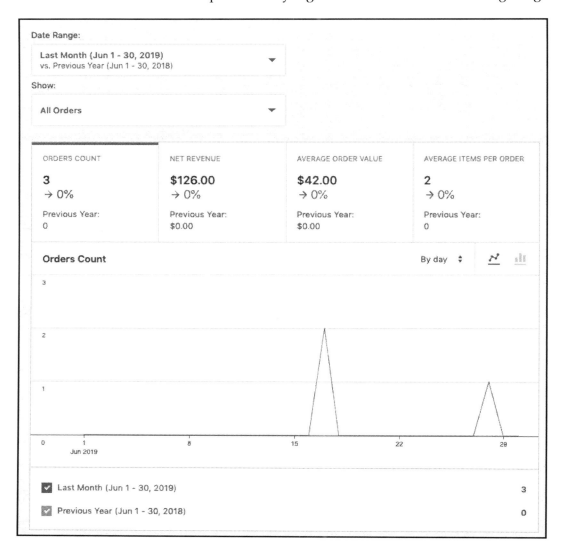

The first element that you notice is the pretty graph. And the graph does a fine job. But the most useful tool on this page is the **Date Range** feature. You can click on this and compare time periods. In most cases, you will want to compare against a previous month, or a previous year.

This is my favorite way to look at all stats. Compare it against a previous time period, and make sure that the graph is going up and to the right. If so, you're doing great. Don't worry about absolute numbers:

We are going to see the following information:

- What sells
- Gross profit
- Taxes

Let's take a look at them, one by one, in the following sections.

What sells

The next two useful graphs are for **Products & Categories** (pictured in the next diagram). These are really good at showing you *what* is selling. You'll want to get more products like those in order to keep up a steady flow of purchases. Here's an example of my category graph:

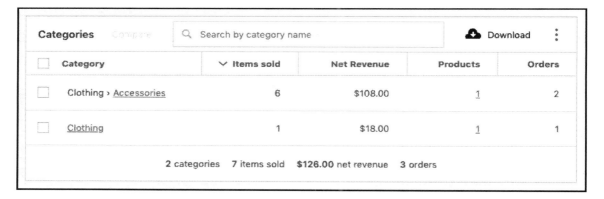

From my example, it seems that clothing accessories, such as hats, sell much better than the clothing itself. I should do more advertising with clothing accessories, and have a wider variety in order to capture even more sales.

Gross profit

One thing that this report doesn't do is show you how profitable an item is. So if you are selling hundreds of products that have a $1 margin, and you sell two items that have a $100 margin, you might actually make more money from the products that you sell fewer of because they have a much higher margin.

This isn't a book on calculating gross profit, but these reports are a great start. You can export to third-party tools, and import the cost of goods numbers. Or, you can look into the WooCommerce Cost of Goods extension (`https://woocommerce.com/products/woocommerce-cost-of-goods/`) to help you with these detail-heavy calculations.

Taxes

The other report that you'll definitely want to familiarize yourself with is the taxes report. This shows you all of the taxes that you have collected, divided by type. So if you collect a state tax, municipality tax, and a county-level tax, all of them will be listed separately, as shown in the following image, so you know exactly where each tax should go:

	Tax Code	Rate	Total Tax	Order Tax	Shipping Tax	Orders
☐	US-CO-CO TAX-1	8.31%	$11.75	$10.48	$1.27	3
	1 tax code		$11.75 total tax	$10.48 order tax	$1.27 shipping tax	3 orders

There are, of course, some third-party tools that do similar things, but it's nice to have a good tax report feature built into WooCommerce. And even if you do use a third-party solution, you can always double-check their numbers with the built-in tool.

Using third-party reporting platforms

There are many services that help with reporting. There are services such as Google Analytics, which help to measure traffic, sessions, and what content users are consuming on your site. And there are services such as Metorik, which add e-commerce data on top of traffic data. We're going to look into Metorik, since it's a business built entirely on top of WooCommerce.

Exploring Metorik

Metorik is built for WooCommerce, and they have very detailed reports that you won't find anywhere else. If you really want to dig into the data of your store in order to make data-informed decisions, Metorik gives you some of the most comprehensive data and visualizations.

They have a free trial, so feel free to explore the service. We can see the dashboard in the next image, and it already gives us tons of information:

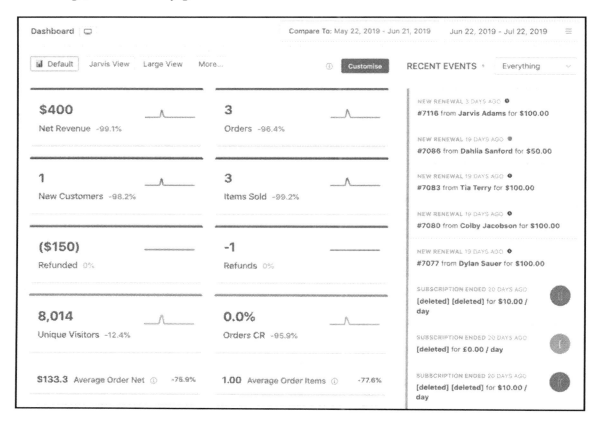

When you log in, you'll see a dashboard with important numbers, often called key performance indicators, or KPIs.

In addition to the standard reports, such as revenue, orders, and refunds, Metorik has a predictive algorithm. You can forecast your sales over months or years, as shown here:

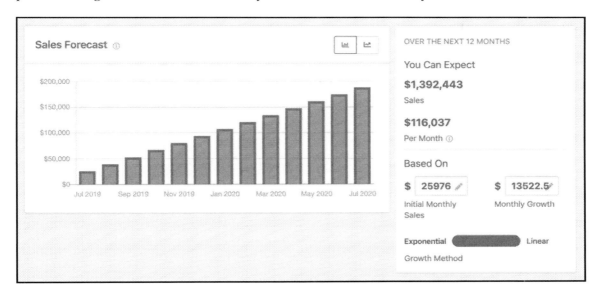

This also applies to subscriptions. And this data is incredibly important. It can calculate for how long customers will be customers (retention rate), as well as when they'll likely stop paying (churn). When you combine these numbers with your subscription price, you can calculate your customer lifetime value, which is basically how much money you'll ever make from a customer:

> **Lifetime**
>
> Based on an **average** monthly subscription retention rate of **-150.0%**, your expected subscription lifetime is **0.4 months**.
>
> In July '19, your average monthly revenue per subscriber was **$100**, giving you an expected subscription lifetime value of **$40**.

When you know your customer lifetime value, you know the absolute maximum that you can spend on a customer and still make money. In the previous example, I could spend $10 on advertising to acquire the customer, spend $20 on the cost of the product itself, and keep $10 in profit.

And if I can extend how long customers will subscribe for, I can keep a lot more of that revenue!

Pick one

There are a lot of great tools out there. You don't need to subscribe to all of them. Pick one, or maybe two tools that give you useful numbers, and stick with them.

Since Google Analytics is the standard tool and it's free, I recommend that you set it up, even if you don't plan on using it. A couple of years from now, if you change your mind, or you have a contractor that needs the tool, you'll be glad you have those years of data.

Summary

Store owners have a lot to do. Some of the most important duties are fulfilling and refunding orders. You might have to do both of these daily, if your store takes off.

But, store owners will also have to review sales data both inside and outside of WooCommerce so that they know which products are selling well, how much their customers are spending, and how long they're customers for.

Now that you know how to do all of these things, you can manage your own online store. In the next chapter, we're going to look into growing your store and syncing data between different storefronts.

6
Syncing Product Data

When you run an online store, it's tempting to list your products on as many stores as possible so that you can get as much revenue as possible. A great example of this gone wrong is when you have a WooCommerce store where you list a kite for $10 and you have an eBay store in which you sell the exact same kite for the same price. If you update one price and forget to update the other, you can run into the following problems:

- You could miss out on additional income.
- Customers could find out they paid a higher price and demand a refund (or, even worse, they refund on one system and rebuy the exact item on your other site).
- You could oversell a product and not have enough stock to fulfill orders.

In general, it's a bad idea to store data in two or more places. You always want to store it in just *one* place. This principle is called the **singular source of truth** (**SSOT**)(https://en.wikipedia.org/wiki/Single_source_of_truth). And the goal is to only ever list a piece of data (such as a product price) in one place and then have every other system talk to your singular source of truth. This prevents a ton of issues where data is outdated.

In this chapter, we're going to look at the following three tools you can use to sync data:

- Exporting data out of WooCommerce
- Importing data into WooCommerce
- Using an **Enterprise Resource Planning** (**ERP**) system

By the end of this chapter, you will be able to make sure your data is stored correctly so you can avoid syncing and inventory problems, as well learning how to import and export data, and how to effectively use the ERP system.

Exporting out of WooCommerce

If you create a brand new company for your store, you might be able to store *all* of your product data in WooCommerce and use it as your singular source of truth. If so, you're lucky.

If you ever need to copy data to another system, you should set up a direct integration, such as the WooCommerce Square integration (which we will set up in the next chapter), that automatically syncs products and product data between both systems. However, if you don't have a direct integration, then you'll need to export data manually under **WooCommerce** | **Products** | **Export** and **Import** it into the new system as follows:

Alternatively, you could use a tool such as Zapier (`https://zapier.com/home`) that lets you connect your WooCommerce store with hundreds of other online applications. You can configure Zapier to watch for product updates and to update another system with each update.

If you use multiple systems to sell your products, you might have to export your product data manually and then load it into the other system. Now you know how to export data, for the rest of this chapter we're going to focus on syncing WooCommerce with these other systems. Let's see how to import products in the following section.

Importing products via CSV

One of my first WooCommerce projects was for a large furniture company who had their own proprietary database where they kept all of their product information. This database was where they added new products, updated the price, and added photos and placed them into categories.

They wanted their website to reflect what was in the database. So, we had two options:

- Integrate with WooCommerce so every database change is mirrored on the website.
- Export products into a **comma-separated values (CSV)**, and import it into WooCommerce.

Functionally speaking, both approaches achieve the same results. But having to maintain integration with an unfamiliar proprietary database sounds like a lot of work and a potential headache. However, exporting products into a CSV file is pretty easy to do, and it's equally easy to import that CSV into WooCommerce.

We're going to look into the data that is stored in a CSV file, how you can determine which data to include in a CSV file, and finally how to import a CSV file into your WooCommerce store.

Exploring a CSV file

Before we go any further, it's worth very briefly explaining what exactly a CSV file is. CSV stands for comma separated values. A CSV file is technically just text. And if you open it up with a text or code editor, you'll see something similar to this:

```
ID,Type,SKU,Name,Published,"Is featured?","Visibility in catalog","Short description",Description,"Date sale price starts","Date sale price ends","Tax status","Tax class","In stock?",Stock,"Backorders allowed?","Sold individually?","Weight (lbs)","Length (in)","Width (in)","Height (in)","Allow customer reviews?","Purchase note","Sale price","Regular price",Categories,Tags,"Shipping class",Images,"Download limit","Download expiry days",Parent,"Grouped products",Upsells,Cross-sells,"External URL","Button text",Position,"Attribute 1 name","Attribute 1 value(s)","Attribute 1 visible","Attribute 1 global","Attribute 2 name","Attribute 2 value(s)","Attribute 2 visible","Attribute 2 global","Meta: _wpcom_is_markdown","Download 1 name","Download 1 URL","Download 2 name","Download 2 URL"
44,variable,woo-vneck-tee,"V-Neck T-Shirt",1,1,visible,"This is a variable product.","Pellentesque habitant morbi tristique senectus et netus et malesuada fames ac turpis egestas. Vestibulum tortor quam, feugiat vitae, ultricies eget, tempor sit amet, ante. Donec eu libero sit amet quam egestas semper. Aenean ultricies mi vitae est. Mauris placerat eleifend leo.",,,taxable,,1,,0,0,,.5,24,1,2,1,,,,"Clothing > Tshirts",,,"https://woocommercecore.mystagingwebsite.com/wp-content/uploads/2017/12/vneck-tee-2.jpg, https://woocommercecore.mystagingwebsite.com/wp-content/uploads/2017/12/vnech-tee-green-1.jpg, https://woocommercecore.mystagingwebsite.com/wp-content/uploads/2017/12/vnech-tee-blue-1.jpg",,,,,,,,0,Color,"Blue, Green, Red",1,1,Size,"Large, Medium, Small",1,1,1,,,,
```

In its raw form, it's not very useful. However, text separated by commas is very easy for a computer to parse, which is why it's such a useful medium for sending data. If you open the same file in a program capable of displaying this information, you'll see something very different. You can see the same CSV file in Numbers (similar to Excel) in the following screenshot:

	ID	Type	SKU	Name	Published	Is featured?	Visibility in catalog	Short description
2	44	variable	woo-vneck-tee	V-Neck T-Shirt	1	1	visible	This is a variable product.
3	45	variable	woo-hoodie	Hoodie	1	0	visible	This is a variable product.
4	46	simple	woo-hoodie-with-logo	Hoodie with Logo	1	0	visible	This is a simple product.
5	47	simple	woo-tshirt	T-Shirt	1	0	visible	This is a simple product.
6	48	simple	woo-beanie	Beanie	1	0	visible	This is a simple product.
7	58	simple	woo-belt	Belt	1	0	visible	This is a simple product.
8	60	simple	woo-cap	Cap	1	1	visible	This is a simple product.

CSV files can very easily be opened by spreadsheet programs such as Microsoft Excel, Numbers, and Google Sheets, and you can easily export a CSV file from any of these programs.

When you make a CSV file, you might be prompted to choose *delimiters* and a few other settings. You should be able to use the defaults. Either way, WooCommerce lets you import any CSV file, and you can customize those settings on import to match your export.

Including content in the CSV file

Figuring out exactly what should be included in a CSV file for products is actually a lot of work. If you try to do it manually, you are likely to make a mistake and have one too many or too few commas, which will mess up the entire import.

To make this easy on yourself, start by exporting the default products in WooCommerce. You can even create a demo product or two, with settings similar to your products and then export those.

You can do this under **WooCommerce** | **Products** | **Export**, as shown in the following screenshot:

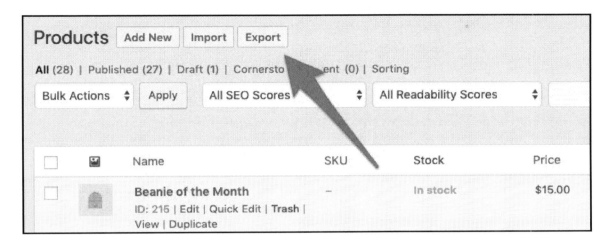

The default options should be good. They are shown in the following screenshot:

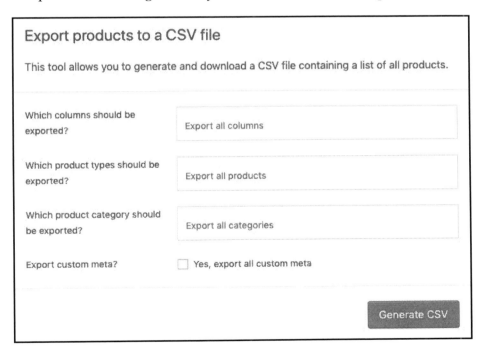

Click **Generate CSV** and now you have a perfect template. You can delete the sample products and replace them with your own products. To make this process a little easier, if you have your own products spreadsheet, rename your columns to match the columns in the WooCommerce CSV export. That way it's dead simple to match columns during the import process.

Importing a CSV

Now that we have a CSV file ready to go, it's time to import that file:

1. We can do this under **WooCommerce | Products | Import**, as shown in the following screenshot:

Now we get to go through the import process.

2. Upload your file and choose whether you want to update existing products. New products will be skipped. This is a nice option when we only have a small selection of products on our site. Otherwise, I recommend leaving this option disabled.

You can see the settings for importing a file in the next screenshot:

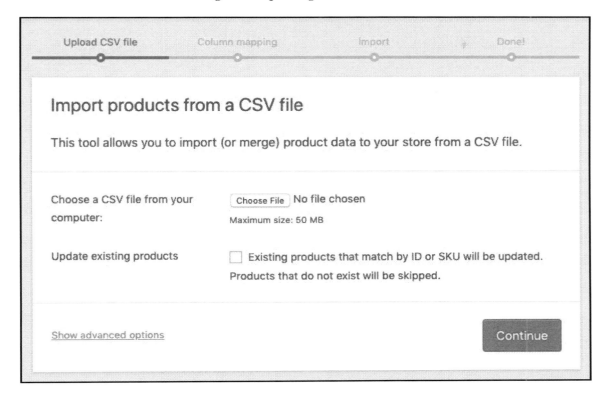

The next step is the most important. Make sure that the data is imported into the right fields. If you used the exported WooCommerce CSV file, this should be pretty easy.

3. Double-check the columns in the CSV (left) match the value in WooCommerce (right), which you can see in the following screenshot:

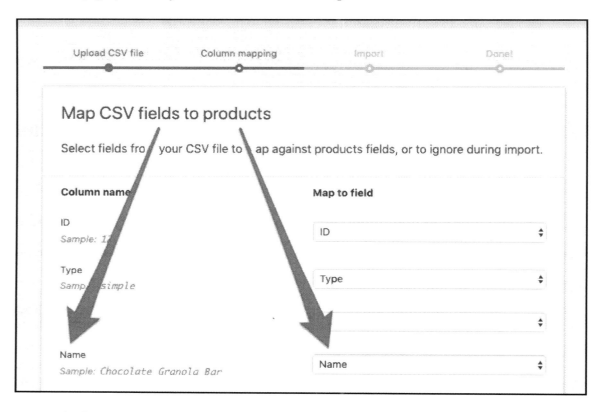

4. Once you match all the columns, you can import the data. Click on **import**.

This might take a while depending on how many products you're importing. And if you link to a bunch of images in the CSV file, they will definitely take some time to import. Once you are done, you should see a screen about the import as follows:

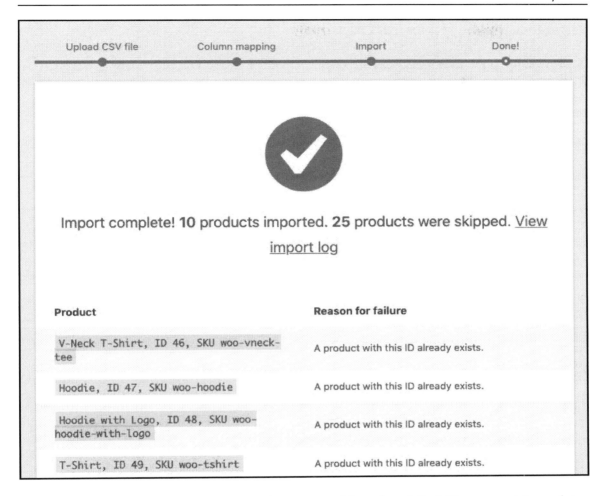

You can view the log and see if any products were skipped or failed. If you want to update products, then you can go back to the beginning and click the checkbox to update existing products.

The trickiest part is making sure your data is mapped to the correct field in WooCommerce. If you can get that part correct, the rest of this process only takes a few minutes and the import will go smoothly.

Understanding ERP

As your store grows, it's natural to slowly piece together different pieces of technology to solve the day-to-day challenges of running a business. You'll likely have different systems for the following:

- Accounting
- Taxes
- Shipping
- Inventory

And this is fine for small stores, but as you grow it becomes a lot to remember. For example, you sell 10 bicycles a month and you have 11 bikes left. A customer buys a bike and WooCommerce sends you a low-stock notification. You go to your vendor and ask for a quote/invoice. You pay the invoice and log it in your accounting system. You receive the bicycles and you have to mark the order as received. Then you log the bicycles into WooCommerce so new users can buy them.

This is a delicate process and breaks the single-source-of-truth principle we talked about earlier because at certain points you have to remember to log the same event in multiple systems.

There is an easier way. You can use an ERP system. These are hubs for your entire business. And they integrate with many different tools so you only have to enter something once and the data gets shared with your other tools.

Let's look at the earlier example again using an ERP: a customer buys a bike and your ERP sends you a low-stock notification. You go to your vendor and ask for a quote/invoice. You log the paid invoice in the ERP. You receive the bicycles and mark the order as received. WooCommerce is automatically updated with the new quantity. Now, since everything is logged in one place, you have accurate numbers for the health of your business (taking into account revenue and costs).

Finding an ERP

There are hundreds of ERPs, and they all focus on different aspects of e-commerce. Some are really good at accounting, some at shipping, and some at managing customers and tracking all data related to the customer.

I tend to value the following two aspects:

- Product information and inventory
- Accounting and purchase orders

If you can tie these two parts of an e-commerce business, it will really help you manage your cash flow and make you more profitable. If you are a marketing wiz, you might want to put all customer information in one place, which can be really useful for maximizing repeat sales and reacquiring customers, both helping your bottom line. And while this is important, I hate drowning in paperwork and misplacing a $1,000 purchase order that wasn't logged in the right place and was never delivered as it had been forgotten about.

Here are just a couple of solutions that I found in my research:

- Tradegecko (https://www.tradegecko.com/)
- Dear Systems (https://dearsystems.com/)
- WP ERP (https://wperp.com/)

We're going to look into Dear Systems since their software pretty easy to use. You may want to do your own research to find the best ERP system for your business and set it up. The steps for setting up your ERP should be similar to what we're going to do.

Understanding Dear Systems

The first thing you're going to have to do with any ERP is to connect it to WooCommerce. In Dear Systems you can connect your store by going to **Integrations** | **WooCommerce** and click the + button, which you can see in the following screenshot:

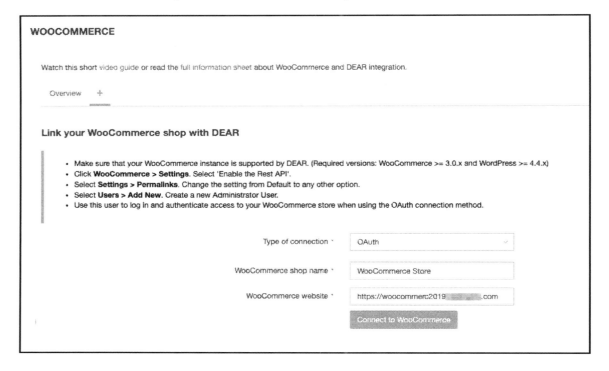

This will use the WooCommerce REST API. By default, this should be enabled. If it's not, then you can enable it under **WooCommerce** | **Settings**. Then you'll be prompted to review the permissions and approve them:

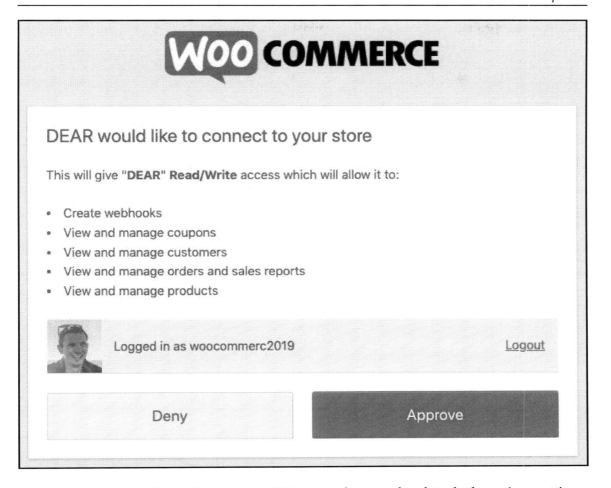

WooCommerce should now be connected. You may have to do a lot of other minor settings. I had to do the following:

- Set a default customer.
- Connect tax rates in WooCommerce to taxes in the ERP.
- Connect payment methods in WooCommerce to payment methods in the ERP.
- Deselect **Use WooCommerce as Master source for DEAR products**.

And there's likely a lot more you'll have to do. ERPs are notorious for being hard to set up (and this is one of the easiest I found). When your functionality is to connect all of your other business tools, it tends to get complicated.

Once you have the integration taken care of, then you can place those purchase orders as shown in the next screenshot:

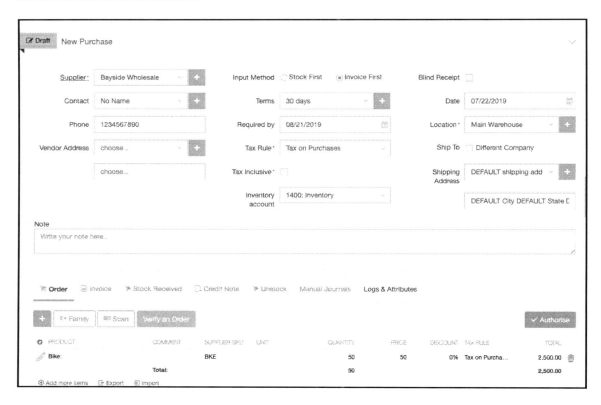

When you mark the purchase order as complete, the inventory will be updated in the ERP, which will be synced with WooCommerce.

Using an ERP

ERPs are very challenging to set up and require a *lot* of technical knowledge. They are amazingly powerful, but take a lot of setup time. They also tend to be expensive software. Many of these platforms are over $100 a month.

I recommend setting one up as soon as you start entering lots of information into multiple systems. When it prevents you from making mistakes or saves hours of data entry, then you'll see it's worth the setup time.

Since ERPs take so long to set up, the switching costs are high—meaning you're very likely to stay with an ERP even if it doesn't do everything you want. For that reason, I recommend you do the research into which ERP is perfect for your company.

Summary

If you only have one store you shouldn't have to worry too much about syncing data between multiple systems. But as your business grows, you'll likely need to share data and if there isn't a direct integration, you'll have to look into other systems and processes, including the ones we looked into this chapter.

In this chapter, we learned how to export and import CSV files from and into your WooCommerce site. That means you can easily connect any system to WooCommerce. We also learned how to use an ERP system that can keep all of our data in one place and should help our business run more efficiently. Now we're ready to share data with other systems.

In the next chapter, we're going to look into using a **point-of-sale** (**POS**) system so that you can sell your products in person.

Configuring In-Store POS Solutions

If you have experience with the retail world, you're probably very familiar with the term POS. It stands for **Point-of-Sale**, and it's the system an employee uses to enter an order.

They usually have a simple touch interface where you tap products, add them to the order and pay for the order. And the POS system usually has the technology to process credit cards. Sometimes, it has more advanced functionality, such as adding a customer to the order so that customer data is synced between your online store and your POS system.

POS systems range in complexity. For a mall kiosk or for selling at a convention, you'll probably want the simplest and most compact POS you can find. A bare-bones POS system will likely have the following two components:

- Credit card reader
- Receipt printer

If you have a department store with dozens of checkout locations, you might want additional functionality:

- A built-in cash drawer
- Barcode scanner
- Employees can clock in/out
- Layered permissions where certain functionality can only be accessed by a manager

Since WooCommerce integrates with so many systems, there are a ton of POS options to choose from. Some of the most popular are as follows:

- WooCommerce POS (`https://wcpos.com/`)
- Square
- Lightspeed

But there are hundreds more you can choose from. Each industry will have its own favorite POS systems based on their unique needs. So. do some digging by searching for `{{your industry}} + POS systems`.

In this chapter, we'll cover the following topics:

- Setting up WooCommerce POS
- Setting up Square
- Syncing data in store and online

By the end of this chapter, you should know how to configure a POS system with your WooCommerce store.

Setting up WooCommerce POS

WooCommerce POS is a plugin built on top of WordPress. It's similar to WooCommerce, the core plugin, which is free and available on GitHub (`https://github.com/kilbot/WooCommerce-POS`). They have premium features that you can unlock by buying a license.

We're going to explore the free version that anyone can experiment with. Follow these steps to set up the POS:

1. In your WooCommerce site, you can go to **Plugins** | **Add New**.
2. Search for `WooCommerce POS`. The plugin is shown in the following screenshot:

3. Now you can install and activate the plugin.

 WooCommerce POS uses the same database as your WooCommerce site. This is great in many ways. But it also means that if you experiment with WooCommerce POS, it's easy to clutter up your database. So, if you experiment with this POS system, I recommend you do so with a test site.

Once you've installed the plugin, you'll see a new item called POS in your admin menu. From there, you can immediately see what it does by clicking **POS** | **View POS**. Here's what it looks like on your screen:

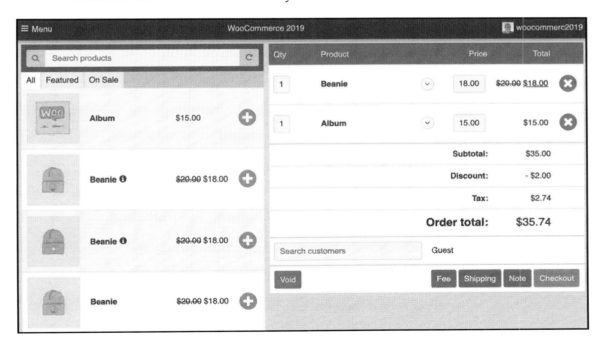

Immediately, we can see the results! Since this plugin is built directly on top of WordPress, with just a couple of clicks, we can see results. We can see a list of products in three categories:

- **All**
- **Featured**
- **On Sale**

We simply click them or search for specific products and we can see the items being added to our cart on the right. We can add a fee, add shipping, and assign this order to a specific customer.

Then, we can click **Checkout**. This is where the platform is a bit limited. Since it lives in the browser, it doesn't have a direct connection to a credit card reader. By default, you can checkout with any of the following:

- PayPal
- Cash
- Debit/credit card (via EFTPOS)

If you're paying with cash, it's very easy. Enter the cash received and the order will be marked as paid. For conventions or farmers' markets, this is super easy. Credit cards are a little more challenging. Let's look at how you can accept credit cards and when you should choose WooCommerce POS.

Accepting credit cards

The most useful feature in a POS system is a card reader. There is a list of card readers in the documentation (https://faq.wcpos.com/v/0.5/en/compatible-credit-card-readers.html). To summarize, you'll have to enter the order total into a separate application, such as Payment for Stripe (https://paymentforstripe.com/card-readers), then swipe the card and mark the order as paid. Let's see how to use Stripe.

Setting up Payment for Stripe

Follow these steps:

1. First, download the Payment for Stripe app on your phone.
2. Open the app and enter the order total, which you can see in the following screenshot:

3. Press the arrow to move to the next step.

4. On the following screen, enter the credit card information or scan a credit card:

5. When you're done, press **Charge** (currently grayed out in the screenshot) and the funds will be transferred.

   Now you can go back to WooCommerce POS, select card as a payment method, and click **Process Payment**.

That's it. If you like this process, you should consider selecting WooCommerce POS as your POS system.

Selecting WooCommerce POS

WooCommerce POS is a little clunky when processing cards. It's obviously nicer to have a built-in terminal that knows the total (so you don't have to re-enter the amount) and logs all the relevant details into the order in your system (so it's easy to link credit card transactions to specific orders).

But the WooCommerce POS system is *incredibly* easy to set up, you don't need any extra accounts, and you can start by manually typing in credit cards immediately, meaning you don't have to get any hardware or pay for *anything*.

WooCommerce POS is the only 100% free option. If you like it, you'll probably want to get the credit card reader even though that is a one-off fee.

If you want a more comprehensive service, then you'll want to look into Square, which we're covering next.

Setting up Square

If you've stepped into a coffee shop in the last decade, you've probably used Square. It's one of the most popular and general-purpose POS systems. It's designed for small businesses and excels at that role. They have competitive pricing and integrations with major platforms, and the product itself is really easy to use.

We'll look into how we can connect our store with Square, set up the integration, and sync data between Square and WooCommerce.

Connecting with Square

To integrate with Square, you need a Square account, and you need to download the free Square extension for WooCommerce (`https://woocommerce.com/products/square/`). Let's start by installing the Square extension for WooCommerce. Once you've installed and activated the plugin on your site, you'll see a notice to configure it, which you can see here:

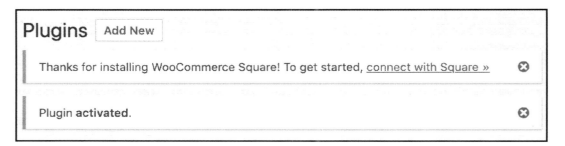

Follow these steps:

1. Click **connect with Square >>**. You'll be redirected to the Square for WooCommerce settings page located at **WooCommerce | Settings | Square**:

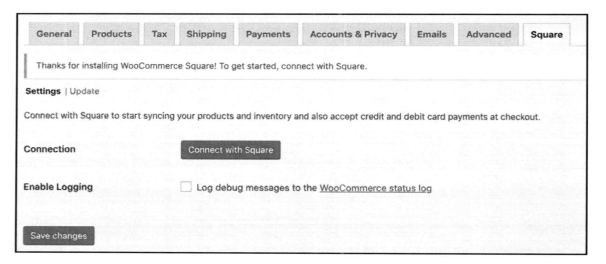

On this page, you'll see a big button to **Connect with Square**.

2. Click on **Connect with Square** and you'll be redirected to your Square account.

3. Log in if you haven't already and you should see a page that describes the permissions that WooCommerce needs to interact with Square, as shown in the following screenshot:

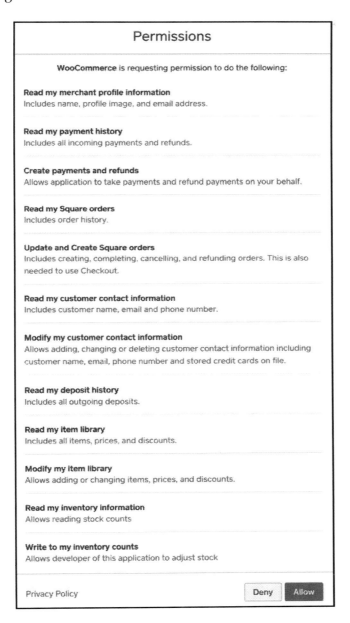

As you can see, the list of permissions is huge. WooCommerce is basically going to manage every aspect of your Square store. To set up permissions, follow these steps:

1. Click **Allow**.
2. On the confirmation page, click the button to be redirected back to your WooCommerce store:

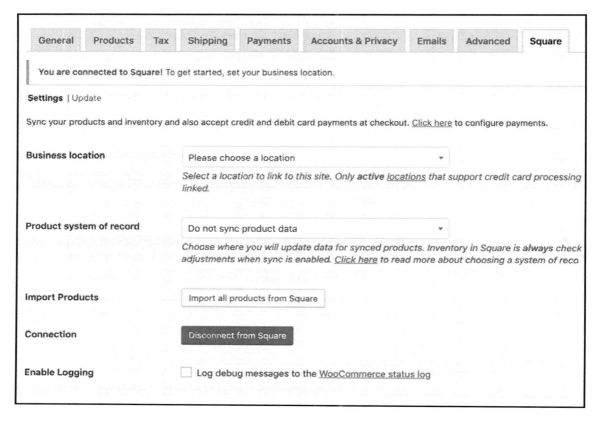

Let's see how to set up Square for WooCommerce in the next section.

Setting up Square for WooCommerce

Now that we've installed and connected Square, we need to adjust a few settings. There are two important aspects that we'll look into:

- Business location
- Product system of record

The business location is a feature of Square (https://squareup.com/help/us/en/article/5580-manage-multiple-locations-with-square). They're designed for multiple physical locations. But they can actually be useful for online stores.

If you store your online store inventory in a warehouse, you can create a new location for that warehouse and it will have a separate inventory than your other stores. Whatever location you select, that is the inventory your WooCommerce store will use.

If everything is stored in one place, then you don't need to create a new location. You can just select the one location you have.

The product system of the record (https://docs.woocommerce.com/document/woocommerce-square/#sync) sounds very technical, but it's actually very simple. Since you have two databases (WooCommerce and Square), WooCommerce needs to know which one is the master.

You can choose three options:

- Do not sync product data
- WooCommerce
- Square

Do not sync product data is the most straightforward. You can have two totally independent systems. If you don't have a lot of overlap between your online store and your brick and mortar stores, this might be a good option for you.

The next option is **WooCommerce**. When WooCommerce is the system of record, your Square product catalog will be overwritten with data from your WooCommerce store for these fields:

- Product name
- Product price
- Inventory count (if inventory sync is enabled)
- Product category
- Product image

The last option is **Square**. When Square is the system of record, your WooCommerce data will be overwritten with data from Square for the following fields:

- Product name
- Product price
- Inventory count (if inventory sync is enabled)
- Product image (if a featured image is not set in WooCommerce)

The system of record only needs to be set once. You don't need to set this setting on a per-product basis.

Once the integration is configured, you'll need to know how the data is synced between the systems.

Syncing data

The option you choose determines how often your data syncs. If Square is the system of record, it updates your WooCommerce store every 60 minutes. If WooCommerce is the system of record, it updates Square immediately, so if a customer places an order, WooCommerce will immediately update the inventory in Square.

We're going to look into how to mark products to sync, when you want to manually sync products, and how the category structures differ.

Marking products to sync

Once you have decided how you want to sync data, you have to mark the products you wish to sync and add an SKU to the products (on the **Inventory** tab). Once you have an **SKU**, you can sync with Square on the **Edit Product** page:

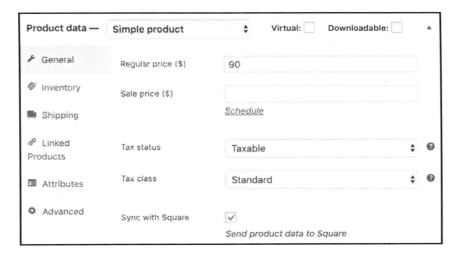

Once you have an **SKU** set under the **General** settings for a product, you can select Sync with Square.

> The SKUs in both systems must match. Otherwise, there will be no data sync.

Manual syncing data

You can always perform a manual sync. Under **WooCommerce | Settings | Square**, click on **Updates** in the submenu, as shown in the following screenshot:

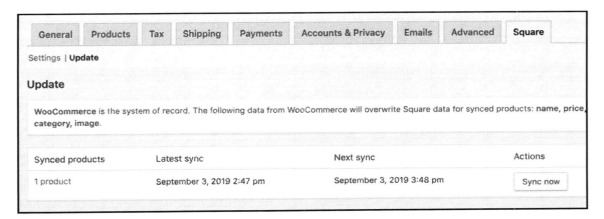

Here, you can see all of the products marked to sync and the last time they were synced.

There's a handy log that notes what happened with each sync. If a product doesn't sync for some reason, you can see it listed here:

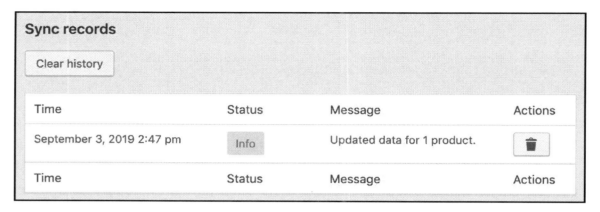

For the most part, you shouldn't need this, but it's always nice to know there's a log in case something doesn't work correctly.

Flat versus hierarchical categories

WooCommerce and Square are very similar, but they do have some differences that are challenging to reconcile. One of those differences is that Square uses a flat category structure like this:

- T-shirts
- Long-sleeved shirts
- Pants
- Shorts
- Capris

However, WooCommerce uses a hierarchical structure like this:

- Shirts:
  - T-shirts
  - Long sleeve shirts

- Pants
- Shorts:
    - Capris

On paper, this looks like a small difference, but it creates huge technical challenges and the integration is limited for these reasons.

Furthermore, Square only allows one category per product, so if your products have multiple categories and sub-categories in WooCommerce, only the first or parent category will be sent to Square. So, if you really want to get the most out of your integration with Square, you are going to have to restructure your categories so the systems can work together.

The systems should now be talking to each other, and all of the data you want to sync should be synced. You can always go into your settings and adjust your settings to add or remove a few products.

Now that we're getting into the complex parts of WooCommerce, it's important to think about how you can sync data between multiple systems.

Syncing data in-store and online

We looked at two very different POS systems in this chapter and they work in very different ways. Square also lets you sync data in a variety of ways, which can be confusing.

It's worth looking into all of the ways you can sync data so you understand which works best for you and your store. We'll look into simple systems such as a single database, having one master database, and manually syncing data.

One database

One of the best systems is to use one database. This is one of the huge advantages of WordPress. There's only one database that all of your plugins use. That means that everything is always up to date. As soon as you have multiple databases, it's possible to have inconsistent data, and using just one database prevents that.

If you're worried about having a perfectly updated database, use a native WordPress solution such as WooCommerce POS.

Mastering synced databases via API

If you have two separate websites that talk to each other (such as Square and your website), there's probably going to be two separate databases talking to each other. In that case, you'll need to have *one source of truth*. One source of truth is an expression in the programming world to stress how important it is to have a primary database and sync all other data from that one source.

If you have multiple sources of truth, there's very likely to be some data loss at some point when syncing. You can have WooCommerce as your one source of truth or another system. It's your choice, and it really comes down to how much you like working with the different systems.

There are sometimes minor incompatibility issues, such as the slightly different category structure in WooCommerce and Square. But for the most part, data should flow pretty easily between both systems.

Manually syncing data

You can, of course, export a CSV from one platform and import it into another platform. I've had to do this on some projects while we were building an automated integration and it gets *very* tedious, *very* fast. And there's always the opportunity for human error.

I don't recommend manually syncing data for an extended period of time. You will eventually forget to sync data or incorrectly sync data and have messed up orders.

Summary

In this chapter, we learned how to set up two different POS systems, one which is built on top of WordPress, and Square, which is its own system with a ton of settings. We also looked into how you can best sync data between systems.

You should now know the basics of setting up a POS system for your WooCommerce store.

In the next chapter, we're going to talk about using fulfillment software to make sending orders much easier.

8
Using Fulfillment Software

In chapter 5, *Managing Sales Through WP-Admin*, we talked about managing orders, and that includes how to mark orders as shipped and how to print out labels through your own site. That's the easiest way to fulfill orders, and that's how I recommend most store owners start.

Once your store starts growing and you need to ship out dozens of packages a day and you have full-time employees helping you send orders, you might want to set up the software to help you ship packages. This is called fulfillment software. Or, you might hire a **third-party logistics partner** (3PL) who will ship your packages for you. These options have numerous advantages:

- You can easily give employees access to fulfillment software so they can do everything in their job (picking and packing items, printing shipping labels, and marking orders as complete) without giving them access to your whole site.
- Most fulfillment software provides built-in shipping discounts, meaning you'll actually save money using this software rather than dropping off packages to the local post office.
- Combine different online stores and marketplaces in one place to make them easy to fulfill.
- 3PLs will do the work for you. You can contract with this company instead of having to rent a warehouse and hire full-time employees to ship packages.

Now that the advantages of using fulfillment software are clear, let's dive deeper into this topic. Through this chapter, we're going to set up several different ways of fulfilling orders. By the end, you should have an easy-to-use system to get packages out the door.

The following topics will be covered in this chapter:

- Sending and updating shipping information
- Configuring Shippo
- Configuring Shipstation

Let's start with sending and updating shipping information in WooCommerce.

Sending and updating shipping information

There are hundreds if not thousands of fulfillment companies. There are a few very well known companies, but there are also hundreds of local fulfillment companies.

The bigger companies that have direct integrations with WooCommerce should automatically retrieve and update order data, but, if you're working with a smaller company, it's important to know what you have to do to send them data and to update data on your end.

We're going to be looking into how you send shipping information to any company and how you can update your own shipping data.

Sending shipping data

Fulfillment companies need data for their job. They need to know who the order is being sent to, their address, what goes in the order, and how they want the order shipped. Without this data, they can't do their job and your packages will just sit in their warehouse.

Some of the biggest fulfillment companies, such as Shippo and Shipstation, have direct integrations with WooCommerce, in which case, install the direct integration and you should be good to go. But if you don't have a direct integration, what can you do?

We're going to look into two solutions that don't require any code, and anyone can implement them. We'll also provide a high-level overview of coding your own solution.

Sending emails

One of the lowest-tech solutions is to send an email to a fulfillment provider. Some 3PLs allow you to send an email. These companies are equipped with software to parse your email searching for important data. They just need the email to include the following details:

- Customer's shipping address and phone number
- Order number
- SKUs and quantities
- How you want to ship the order (such as priority mail or overnight)

This is a pretty low-tech solution, and something you're more likely to see at a local logistics company. They'll keep track of the labor and send you a bill every month. What's great is you don't have to customize your emails from WooCommerce. They already have all of the essential information.

You can go to **WooCommerce** I **Settings** I **Emails** I **New Order** and then click **Manage**. From here, you can CC as many email addresses as you like. This can be seen in the following screenshot:

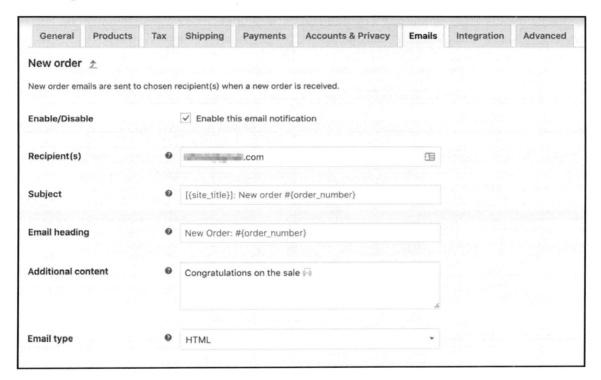

If your fulfillment company wants help parsing your email, you can change the email type from HTML to text. That will help them dissect the email to pull out the relevant details.

When you're done, click **Save** and all of the emails will be sent to your fulfillment company's admin.

Configuring webhooks

A solution that is a bit more programmatic and reliable is using webhooks. If you haven't used webhooks before, they're basically a notification system. So, whenever a specific action happens on your site, a webhook will send some data to a destination. In our case, whenever an order is placed we want to send the order data to a fulfillment partner.

How is this different to an email? Webhooks send data formatted in a specific way that any programming language can parse automatically. This is in contrast to emails, which are formatted for humans. Email parsing programs are complex and can make mistakes. Webhooks are made for programming languages and are far more reliable.

You can go to **WooCommerce | Settings | Advanced | Webhooks** to get started. Then click the **Create a new webhook** button. This can be seen in the following screenshot:

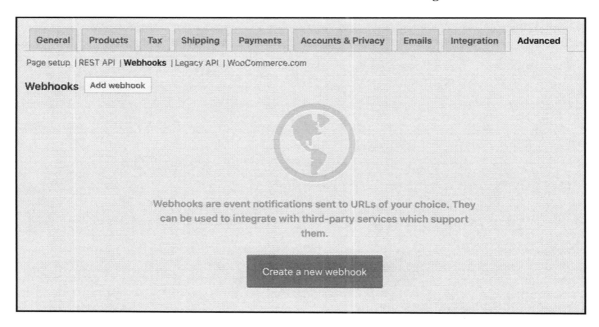

From here, you'll need to configure the webhook. The configuration can be seen in the following screenshot:

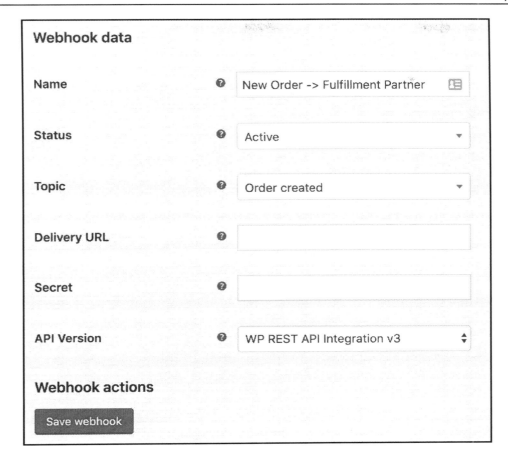

You'll need to give it a name to help you remember what the webhook does. Set the **Status** to **Active**, and for the **Topic**, you'll want to set it to **Order created**.

You'll need to get the **Delivery URL** and **Secret** from your logistics partner. Then save the webhook, and your data will automatically be sent to the partner.

Don't forget to get the delivery URL from your fulfillment partner. They have to provide an inbox for this data, otherwise it won't do anything. Once you save the webhook, all-new order data will be sent to your fulfillment partner and they can begin fulfilling orders immediately.

There is one downside with webhooks. They only send the data once. If your fulfillment company's system is down for maintenance or for some other reason, they might miss the notification. It's rare but it can happen, which is why you might want to look into a custom integration.

Building a custom integration

One of the best things about WooCommerce is that it's open source technology, and you can easily build your own integrations. Building an integration means you're writing your own code to interact with WooCommerce's code and you're sending that information to a new destination.

You can build a solution that sends order data to a fulfillment partner's API. This is what the major shipping logistics companies do. You can browse through the code in the Shippo and Shipstation plugins to see how they send data to their own APIs.

This is very likely going to be a several days or week-long project, so we can't go into the details here. But there are plenty of resources on building your own WooCommerce extensions.

Building integration is an ambitious process. It doesn't take a lot of code, but you have to be comfortable enough with WordPress and WooCommerce to dig into the code to know exactly what you need to write. It is the most robust process. If you plan on building your livelihood on your store, you should at some point work on a thorough integration.

Updating data

We talked about all the ways you can send data to logistics partners but, we didn't talk about how you can update data on your own site. Some store owners don't update their own data. They send order information off to a 3PL and hope they ship everything correctly.

This *can* work, but, when customers write in with their questions about their missing order, how do you handle that? You now have to rely on a third party who may or may not be great at responding to email.

It's a good idea to track all of the data on your own site as well.

At a minimum, you'll want to track:

- Order number
- Order status
- Tracking number

This data will help you answer any customer service question. Let's talk about two different ways you can get this information from a third party.

Processing a daily email

The lowest-tech solution is that some fulfillment companies will send you a daily email with the orders fulfilled along with their tracking numbers.

You could manually update all of this information in WooCommerce. Depending on how many orders are shipped a day, this could be a pretty big time commitment.

However, the benefits outweigh the time commitment because, when you have this data in one place, you can answer any customer support question and you will have access to better/more useful reports through WooCommerce.

Retrieving order data through a custom integration

An idea to save you a lot of manual processing time and reduce human error is to update your custom integration. If the logistics partner has an API, you can write your own integration to check the status of your orders every hour and update them in WooCommerce.

This will take some time to build but will save you countless hours throughout the year. And again, this is one of the main advantages of WooCommerce. Everything is open and customizable; you can build all of the tools you need.

We looked at several low-tech as well as high-tech solutions to sending and receiving data from fulfillment partners. If your fulfillment partner doesn't have a direct integration, you'll have to go with one of these. Pick one and get everything connected so you can make your business more efficient.

Let's now see how to print labels for our orders by using Shippo in the next section.

Configuring Shippo

Shippo is a platform that helps you quickly print cost-effective shipping labels. While platforms such as WooCommerce have done a good job of optimizing printing shipping labels one at a time, companies such as Shippo who specialize in shipping have a whole bunch of extra features:

- Printing batches of shipping labels
- Automating return labels
- Getting pricing discounts for shipping labels

Most fulfillment software charges a monthly fee, but Shippo has a freemium model so you can sign up for free, try it out, and see if it's right for you.

We're going to sign up for Shippo and then show you how to fulfill orders with Shippo.

Signing up for Shippo

Shippo makes it easy to sign up for their service. They have a free account that only takes a moment to set up. Let's set one up. Follow these steps:

1. Start by creating a free account on Shippo.
2. Once you've created your account, Shippo will ask you what platform you're using, as shown in the following screenshot. Click on **WooCommerce**:

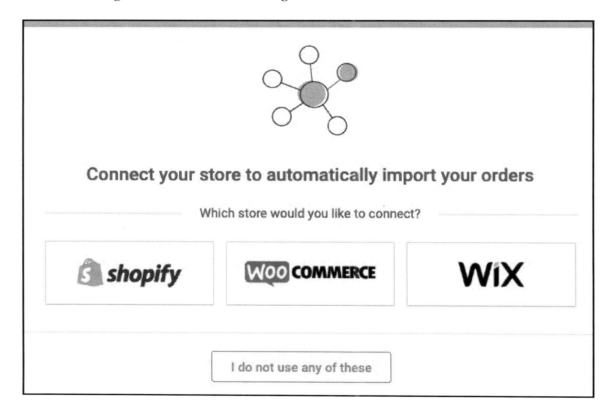

You'll be redirected to a wizard to help you connect your WooCommerce store to Shippo which you can see below:

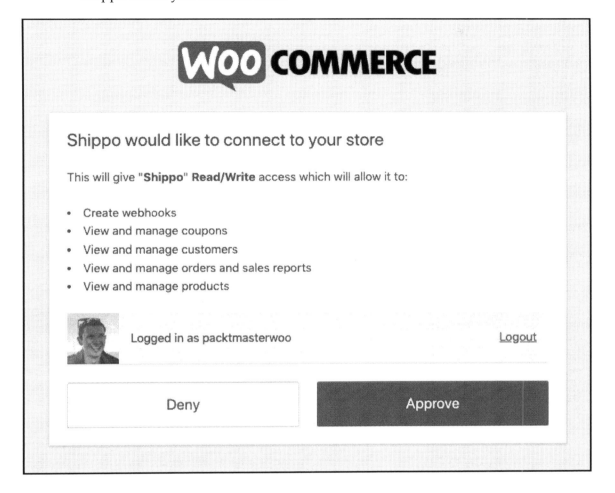

3. Fill out the information in this wizard, specifically the **Store URL** and the **Store Name**. Then click **Connect with WooCommerce**:

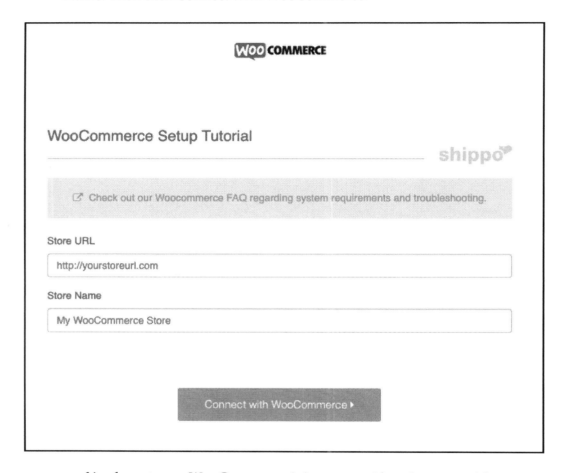

 You have to use WooCommerce 2.6 or newer. If you're on an older version of the plugin, you can't connect to Shippo. When you're connecting to your store, make sure you use HTTPS or HTTP appropriately. If you try to enter an HTTP URL for a site that requires HTTPS, you might not be able to connect.

4. When you click **Connect with WooCommerce**, you'll be redirected back to your site, and you have to grant access.

5. Click Approve in the confirmation box below. Once you do this, your WooCommerce store and Shippo will be connected.

6. Import orders to Shippo by clicking **Sync Orders** in Shippo, which we can see in the following screenshot:

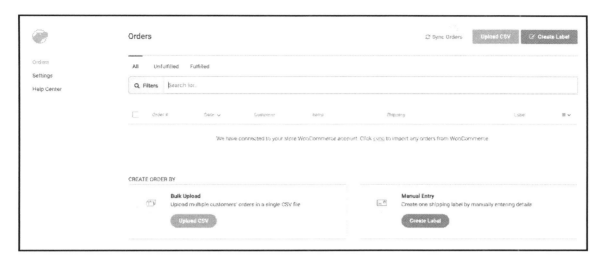

Once you do this, you'll see your orders imported, which can be seen in the following screenshot:

If you're not using a live store, you'll want to make some test orders so you can see orders in Shippo and continue this chapter.

Configuring Shippo setup information

This isn't a book about Shippo, so we're not going to cover every single step. But you'll want to configure a few more things:

- Default sender address
- Add payment information
- Package sizes

You'll need all of these to actually print shipping labels through Shippo. They have a useful help section that you can use to help you finish the setup (`https://support.goshippo.com/hc/en-us`).

Fulfilling orders with Shippo

Once you're fully set up with Shippo, it can make fulfillment much faster. As a simple example, if you pack 10-20 packages from the previous day, you can greatly speed up your efficiency by printing packing slips.

Let's print packing slips in Shippo. Follow these steps:

1. First, go to your dashboard in Shippo.
2. Click on **Unfulfilled**, as shown in the following screenshot. You'll see all of the orders that need to be shipped:

3. Select all of these orders, and you'll see a new option at the bottom of the screen for all selected orders labeled **Download packaging slips for selected orders**, which can be seen in the following screenshot:

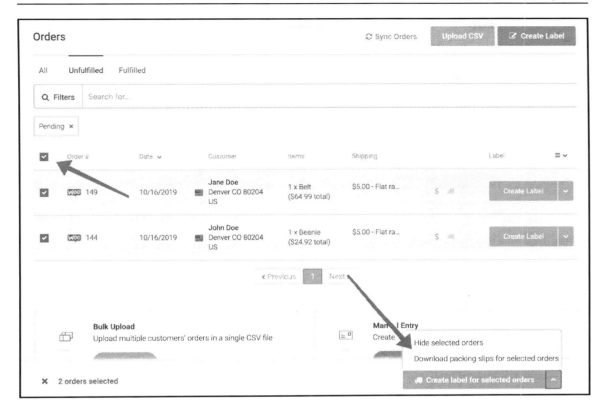

4. Click **Download Packing Slips** and you'll get a PDF with all packing slips. They'll look like this:

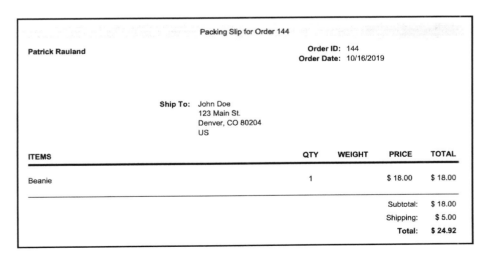

Once you have all of your packing slips printed, you can lay them out and use them to gather all of the items for all of the orders.

Once you've gathered all of your items and put them into your boxes with the help of your packing slips, it's time to print your shipping labels. Follow these steps:

1. Let's select all shipping orders, just like we did with packing slips.
2. Click **Create a label for selected orders**, as seen in the following screenshot:

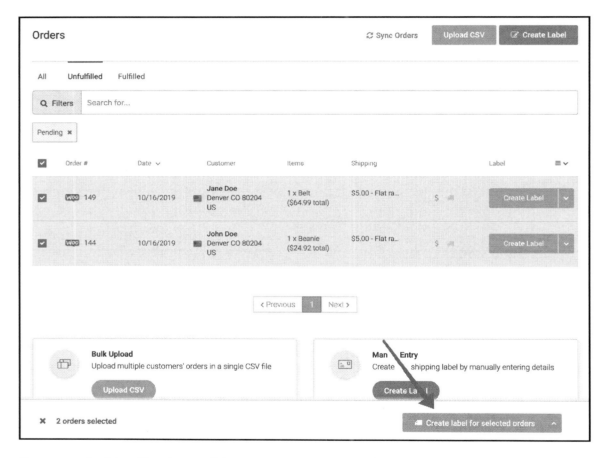

Once you do this, all orders will be updated in Shippo and all shipping information will be sent back to your WooCommerce site.

With that, we've learned how you can connect your store to Shippo, how you can easily view unfulfilled orders, and how you can fulfill them with Shippo.

Now that we know how to print labels using Shippo, let's look into one more popular fulfillment company, called ShipStation.

Configuring ShipStation

In this section, we're going to configure one of the more robust fulfillment platforms, which is ShipStation. This is a fulfillment company that offers similar functionality to Shippo. Their software is more complex. That means it's more powerful and you can do more with it, but it's a little harder to learn to use. They also have a convenient app that makes it easier to fulfill things on the fly.

If you want to have some of the best fulfillment software in the industry and you're willing to pay for it, you'll definitely want to look into ShipStation.

We're going to set up Shipstation to handle our store's fulfillment. Specifically, we're going to do the following:

- Integrate our WooCommerce store with ShipStation
- Print packing lists
- Print shipping labels
- Use the Shipstation app

The first thing we have to do is integrate our store with ShipStation.

Integrating with ShipStation

ShipStation has a 30-day free trial that you can use to get started. Once you sign up for an account, you'll have to do the following:

- Integrate your selling channel (your store)
- Select a shipping carrier
- Configure your label layout
- Add your ship from location

We can see some of these in the following screenshot:

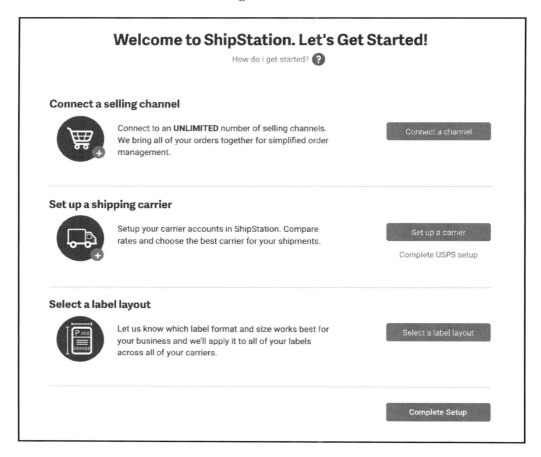

We'll start by integrating with our **selling channel**, or as we call it in this book, our online store. Follow these steps:

1. Click **Connect a channel**, as shown here:

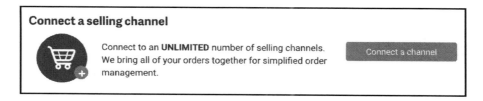

2. Choose **WooCommerce**, as shown here:

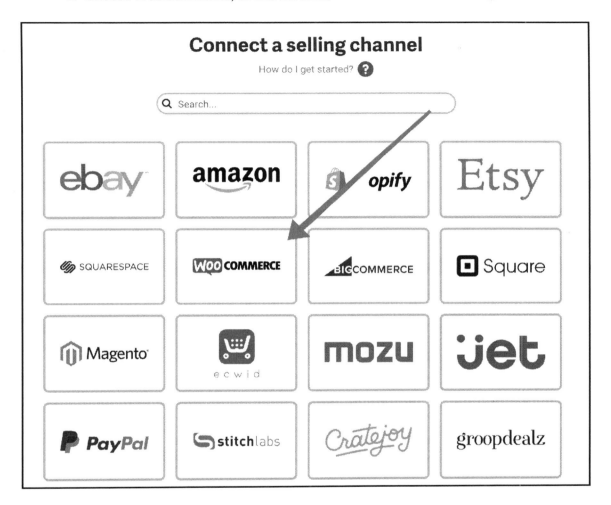

3. Download the ShipStation Integration plugin from WooCommerce, as shown in the following screenshot:

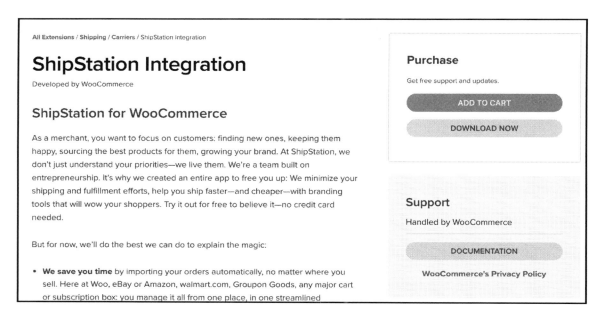

4. Upload the plugin to your WooCommerce site through the plugin uploader.
5. Activate the plugin, and you'll see the following screen:

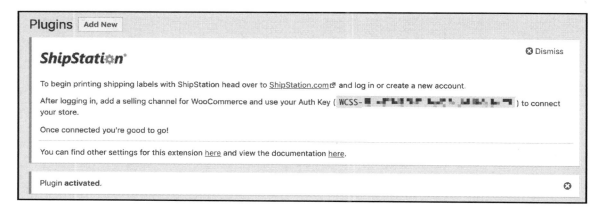

6. Copy the Auth Key on that page into ShipStation, as shown in the following screenshot:

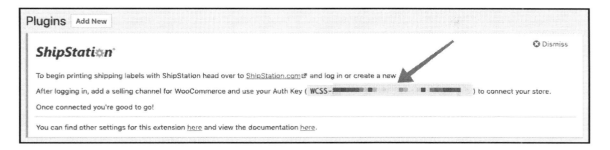

7. Add your URL to ShipStation, as shown in the following screenshot:

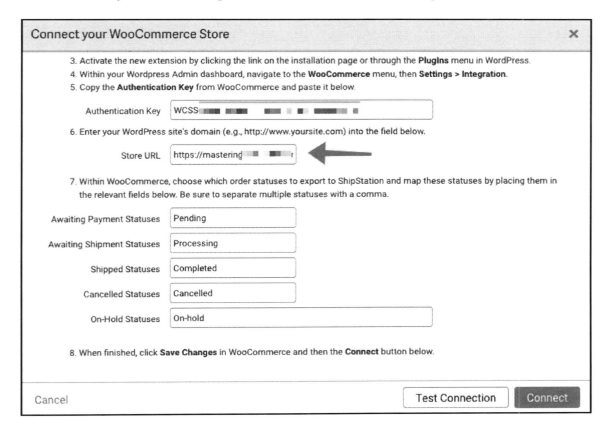

8. Click **Connect**, and you should see a success message like this:

From here, you can add more sales channels (additional WooCommerce stores, Amazon, Etsy, and so on) or continue to set up ShipStation.

We won't cover every aspect of ShipStation, but you will have to configure a specific shipping carrier, configure your shipping labels, and add a shipping address.

Fulfilling packages with ShipStation

Once you've connected your sales channels with ShipStation, you'll see all of your orders from all of your channels in one place. This can be seen in the following screenshot:

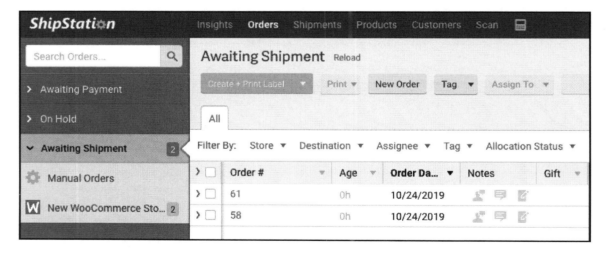

If you click on an order, you can see all of the order details. On the right side, you can configure your shipment. You can add the weight, select the package and the service, and then create and print the label. We can see this in the following screenshot:

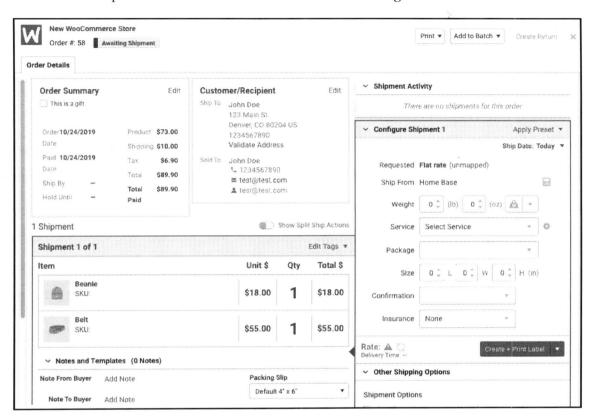

If you select multiple orders, you'll see a different screen where you can validate addresses, which can be super helpful. I've had users give me the wrong address, but this can often be caught with this feature. It prevents orders from going missing, which saves you money, as we can see in the following screenshot:

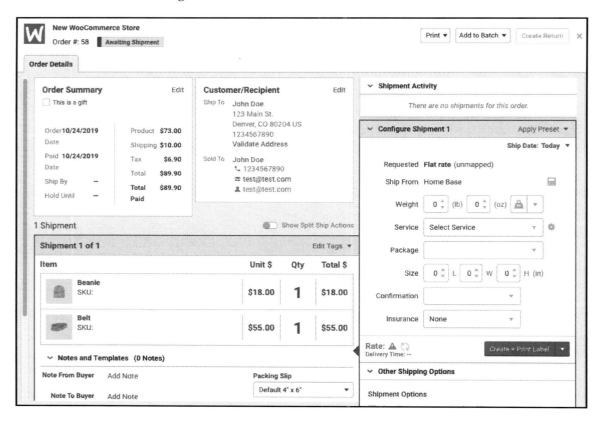

You can also print out the packing slips:

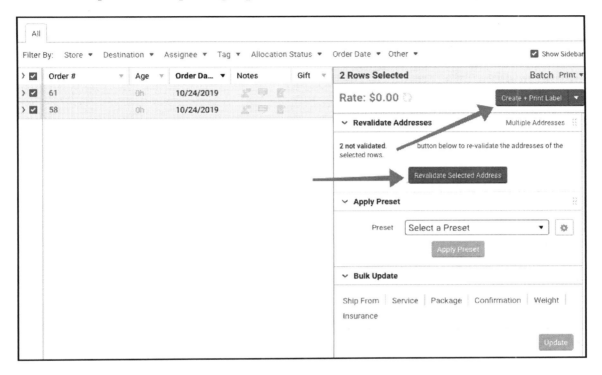

Once you print the shipping labels, the order should be marked as shipped and all shipment information passed back to the original sales channel.

Printing pick lists

If you have a lot of SKUs in your warehouse, it can also be helpful to print pick lists. You print these out and give them to members so they can get dozens of items at a time from the warehouse shelves. They list the warehouse location, which can be very helpful for large catalogs. Follow the steps given below:

1. Select the orders you want to ship. Then click on **Print** at the top of the page, and select **Pick List** from the dropdown, which we can see in the following screenshot:

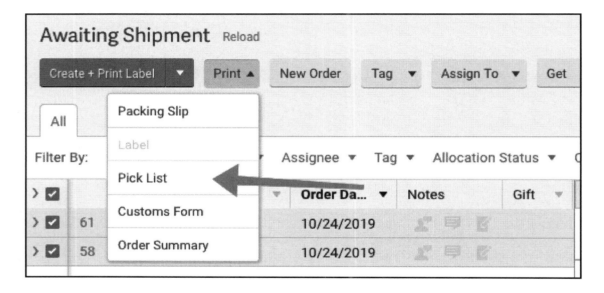

2. You can then print out the pick list, which should look similar to this:

	Item #	Description	Warehouse Location	# Required
		Beanie		1
		Belt		1
		Long Sleeve Tee		1
		Hoodie with Zipper		1
		Polo		1
		Vneck Tshirt		1
		Tshirt		1

Product Pick List

Thursday, October 24, 2019 1:22 PM

Total Items Required: 7

With this handy slip of paper, we can navigate through the warehouse much faster and make fewer trips because there will be fewer errors.

Using the ShipStation app

One of the really nice features of ShipStation is that there is an app. If you don't have to print out a bunch of paper out every day to ship your packages, you can use the app. You can view orders, as shown in the following screenshot:

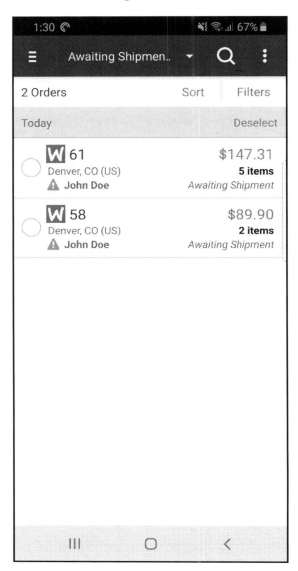

You can also select multiple orders and view or print packing slips and pick lists:

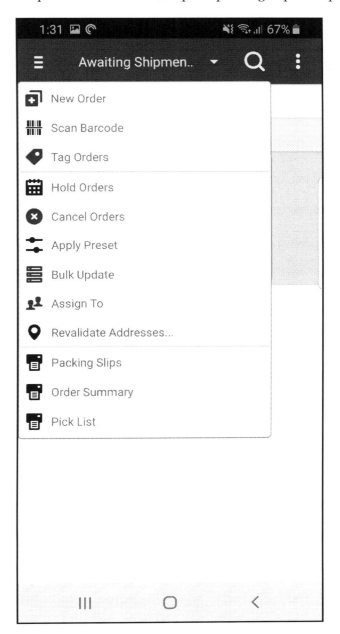

And you can view those pick lists on your device. This is what I see on my phone:

Product Pick List

Thursday, October 24, 2019 1:31 PM

	Item #	Description	Warehouse Location	# Required
		Beanie		1
		Belt		1
		Long Sleeve Tee		1
		Hoodie with Zipper		1
		Polo		1
		Vneck Tshirt		1
		Tshirt		1

Total Items Required: 7

ShipStation is incredibly powerful fulfillment software. If you grow your company to the point where you have a huge inventory, huge staff, or if you just need additional tools, then ShipStation is a great option.

Summary

Fulfilling orders is a fundamental part of eCommerce. Unless you're only selling digital goods, you'll have to create and optimize your own fulfillment process.

You should now be able to send order information to third parties, and you have both high-tech and low-tech solutions. You can integrate Shippo with your online store and fulfill orders through their interface and integrate ShipStation with your online store, create pick lists, fulfill orders, and use their handy mobile app.

With the tools and techniques mentioned in this chapter, handling fulfillment for your store should be much easier.

In the next chapter, we're going to look into speeding up your store.

9
Speeding Up Your Store

When you're running any sort of website, speed is important. But this is even more important with e-commerce where users are browsing pages, adding items to their cart, filling out checkout fields, and, most importantly, paying you.

To illustrate just how important this is, take a look at this statistic: *53% of mobile users leave a site that takes longer than three seconds to load.*

That's over half of your audience. And if you're not careful, your site can take much longer than three seconds to load. Another statistic: *A one-second delay can reduce conversions (sales) by 7%.*

If your store makes $100,000 a year and it slows down by just one second, you'll lose $7,000. For these reasons, it's incredibly important to have a website that loads quickly.

In this chapter, we're going to make sure your site loads fast. We're going to start by showing you how to monitor speed and performance. Then we're going to learn how to minify assets such as CSS and JavaScript files. We'll look into a bunch of ways to optimize images. We'll investigate caching and how much it helps with e-commerce, and lastly, we'll look into optimizing content above the fold (the content you see first).

The following topics will be covered in this chapter:

- Monitoring speed and performance
- Minifying CSS and JavaScript resources
- Optimizing images
- Caching and e-commerce
- Optimizing content above the fold

By the end of this chapter, you should know how to monitor the speed of your site and have a variety of techniques to help you speed it up.

Monitoring speed and performance

Before we can start improving the performance of our site, we need to understand how fast our site is loading and where there might be opportunities for improvement. Without these tools, you're just guessing what will speed up your store, which is super inefficient. You really want to use these tools to track each change you make to ensure it actually speeds up your store.

There are a few free tools we can use to help:

- GTMetrix (`https://gtmetrix.com`)
- Google Page Speed Insights (`https://developers.google.com/speed/pagespeed/insights/`)

In this book, we're going to use GTMetrix, but you can choose another tool if you like.

We're going to create a starting point, test changes, look into waterfall data, and finally set up periodic reports.

Finding a starting point with GTMetrix

Before we start changing things with our site, let's find a starting point. As mentioned earlier, we're going to use GTMetrix. It's a free tool that shows you exactly how fast your page loads, and it also shows where any slow issues might come from.

Perform the following steps given:

1. Register for a free account on GTMetrix (`https://gtmetrix.com`). This will make sure your tests are prioritized over anonymous users, and more importantly you'll be able to set up automatic tests and compare your speed against previous time periods.
2. Copy the URL for your site.

3. Paste it into the URL field on the GTMetrix home page, as shown in the following screenshot:

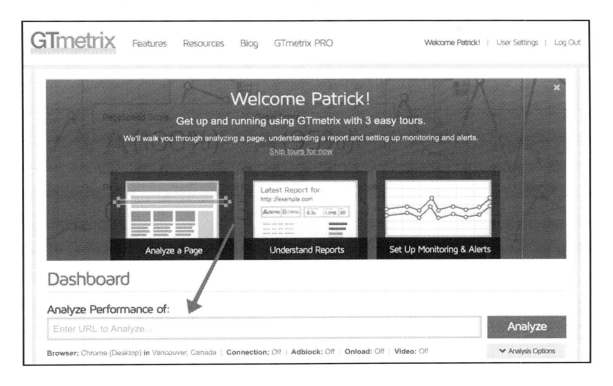

4. Click the **Analyze** button, and it will start analyzing the URL, as seen in the following screenshot:

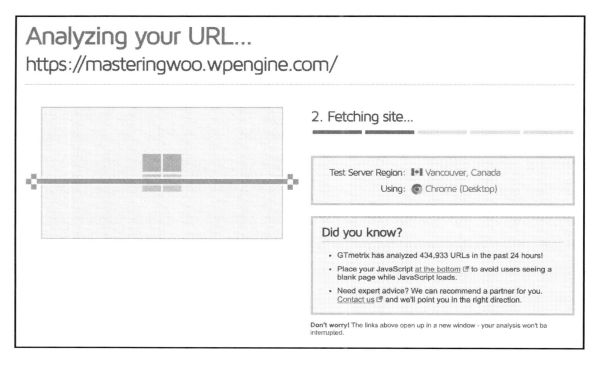

5. After a minute or so, you should get a report.

   There's lots of useful information on the report page. But some of the most useful data is the total time to load and the total size of your web page, which can be seen in the following screenshot:

Latest Performance Report for:
https://masteringwoo.wpengine.com/

Report generated: Thu, Oct 31, 2019 9:35 AM -0700
Test Server Region: Vancouver, Canada
Using: Chrome (Desktop) 75.0.3770.100, PageSpeed 1.15-gt1.2, YSlow 3.1.8
Additional tips: Optimize WordPress, Use a CDN

Performance Scores

PageSpeed Score	YSlow Score
A (93%) ^	C (79%) ^

Page Details

Fully Loaded Time	Total Page Size	Requests
2.8s ^	318KB ^	40 ^

PageSpeed | YSlow | Waterfall | Timings | Video | History

RECOMMENDATION	GRADE	TYPE	PRIORITY
▾ Inline small JavaScript	D (67)	JS	HIGH
▾ Inline small CSS	A (92)	CSS	HIGH
▾ Defer parsing of JavaScript	A (92)	JS	HIGH
▾ Minify CSS	A (94)	CSS	HIGH
▾ Minify JavaScript	A (99)	JS	HIGH
▾ Minify HTML	A (99)	CONTENT	LOW
▾ Avoid bad requests	A (100)	CONTENT	HIGH
▾ Avoid landing page redirects	A (100)	SERVER	HIGH

What do my scores mean?

Rules are sorted in order of impact upon score
Optimizing rules at the top of the list can greatly improve your overall score.

Not every recommendation will apply to your page
The recommendations are meant to be generic, best practices; some things will be out of your control (eg. external resources) or may not apply to your page.

Learn more about PageSpeed/YSlow scores and how they affect performance.

It's incredibly challenging to get a perfect score with an e-commerce site. Don't worry about trying to solve every issue. Focus on the biggest issues, and make incremental progress.

Now that we know our baseline is **2.8** seconds, we can test how new functionality affects our speed.

Testing changes

If we want to add some functionality to our WooCommerce store, we can test it against our baseline (as determined in the previous section).

I currently have the default **Shop** page in WooCommerce as my home page, which displays 12 products. Here is a screenshot of my home page:

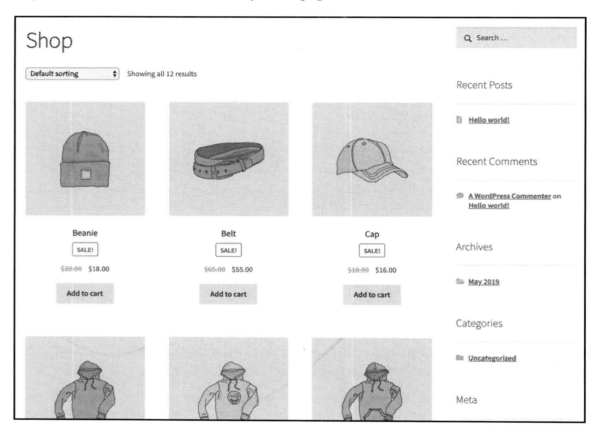

If I want to replace the default page with a custom home page with banners, highlighting specific products, showing off one product in detail, and displaying a few on-sale products at the bottom, what sort of effect will it have?

I created a custom home page with banners and featured products, as follows:

I honestly don't know the effect this has, which is why I want to test it. I went into GTMetrix and tested my new home page. The results can be seen in the following screenshot:

The total time for the site to load increases from **2.8** to **3.1** seconds.

And the total page size increased from **318** to **512 KB**.

Now I can make an educated decision as to whether the change is worth it. If I lose a fraction of my audience over the slightly longer page load, will it be offset by the hopefully higher number of people that will convert with the nicer and more helpful page?

Digging into Waterfall data

If you're not happy with page speed and want to see where the problem is, you can dig into a number of areas in tools such as GTMetrix and Google Page Speed Insights. One tool in GTMetrix is the Waterfall, and it shows you exactly how each resource is loaded.

Just beneath where you see your performance scores and page details with the fully loaded time and total page size, you'll see a list of tabs.

Click **Waterfall,** and you'll see how each resource is loaded, as follows:

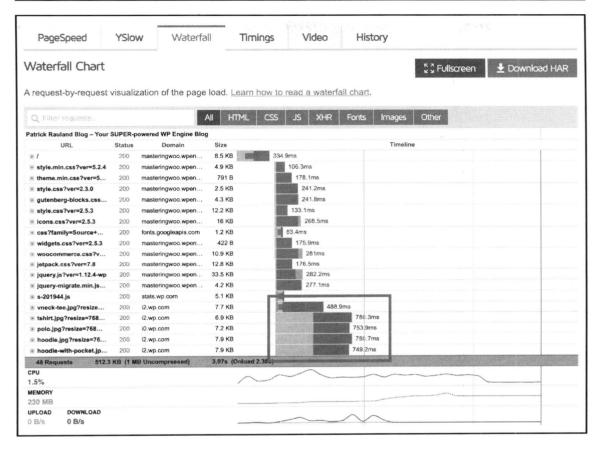

Longer bars mean a resource takes longer to load.

You might notice that, before we can load any assets (images, CSS, JS, and so on) we have to load the page itself. In our diagram, that's represented by "/" since it's the root of the site.

The page tells the browser which additional files to download. If this part is slow (taking over one or two seconds), it's very likely due to a slow or improperly configured server. Contact your host to see how they can help you load the page faster.

In our case, we can see that the images are what is slowing down the page—this isn't too surprising, and is something we're going to optimize later this chapter. But it's nice to see that it's not something else. We know that, we can reduce the number of images, optimize the images themselves, or serve smaller images, we can probably speed up our site.

Setting up periodic testing

I generally recommend testing your page speed when adding new functionality to your site. That said, it's always nice to have records of your page speed over time. For that reason alone, it's worth setting up automatic periodic testing. Without any prompting from you, GTMetrix will test your sites and compare them against previous records.

Let's configure periodic testing in GTMetrix. Perform the following steps:

1. Click on **Monitor** at the top of the test results page, as shown in the following screenshot:

2. Choose how often you want GTMetrix to test your site. I recommend either weekly or monthly:

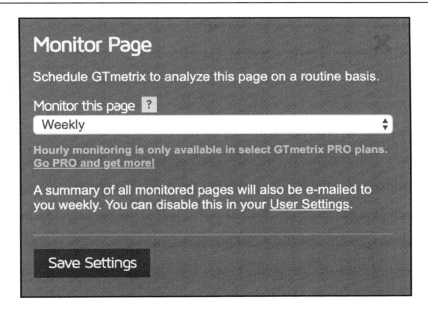

3. Click the **History** tab, and you'll be able to see how the speed of your site changes over time:

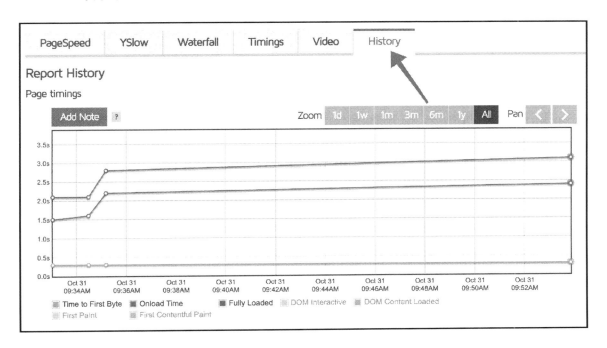

This won't be super useful now since you have only just built the site. But as you gradually add content, update settings, and add new functionality, you'll likely see changes in your page speed, and this tool can help you track how it affects the end user.

Now that we know how to track and monitor our site speed, we'll look into minimizing some resources so our site loads faster.

Minifying CSS and JavaScript resources

One of the easiest ways to get a faster site is to minify your files. You can think of minification as being like reducing the margins on a Word document. You can literally get more words on the page so it takes fewer pages to print. We do that with our files such as CSS, JavaScript, and HTML.

There are a few tools that can do that for us:

- WP Rocket (https://wp-rocket.me)(paid)
- W3 Total Cache(https://wordpress.org/plugins/w3-total-cache/)(free)
- WP Super Minify (https://wordpress.org/plugins/wp-super-minify/)(free)
- Autoptimize (https://wordpress.org/plugins/autoptimize/)(free)

And there are even more than this. There are loads of options to help speed up your site. We're going to use Autoptimize because it's very simple to set up and there's lots of room to customize advanced settings once you know what you're doing.

Let's set up Autoptimize. Perform the following steps:

1. Log into your site and navigate to **Add Plugins.**
2. Click **Add new** and search for **Autoptimize**. Click on **Install Now**:

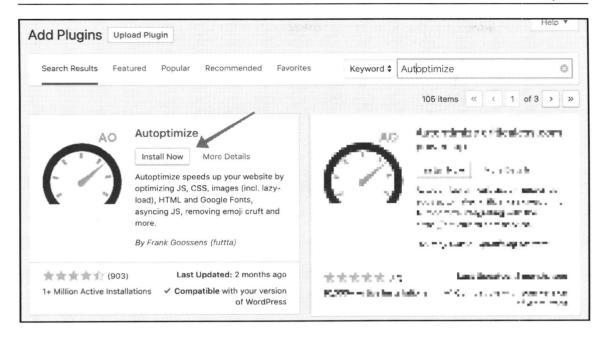

3. Install and activate the plugin.
4. Click on **Settings | Autoptimize** in the admin menu, and you'll see all of the settings.
5. If this is your first time using this plugin, I recommend clicking **Hide advanced settings** as shown in the following screenshot:

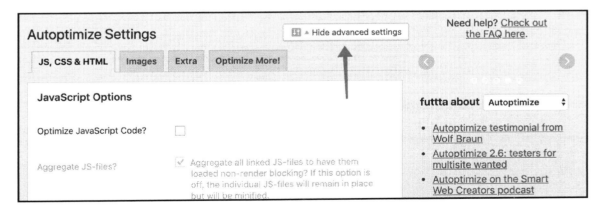

6. Check the checkboxes for optimizing HTML, CSS, and JavaScript as shown in the following screenshot:

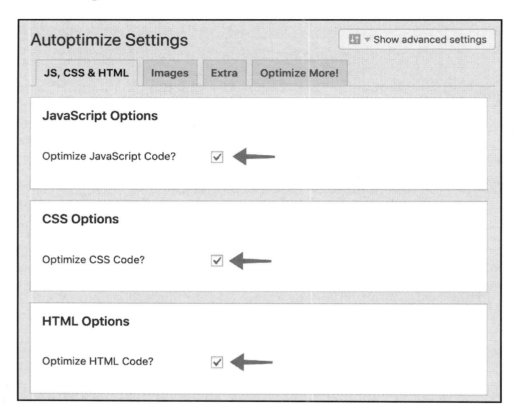

7. Click **Save Changes and empty cache**.

 With any sort of optimization plugin, you have to test after you make any changes. Developers write code in all sorts of different ways, and sometimes a specific plugin or theme can't be optimized automatically; it might break the frontend of your site.

If you do have problems, then you can open up the advanced settings or you can only minimize certain files. For example, you could only minimize HTML and CSS without minimizing JavaScript. I tested my site, and everything seemed to load correctly. So I ran another speed test on GTMetrix. The details can be seen in the following screenshot:

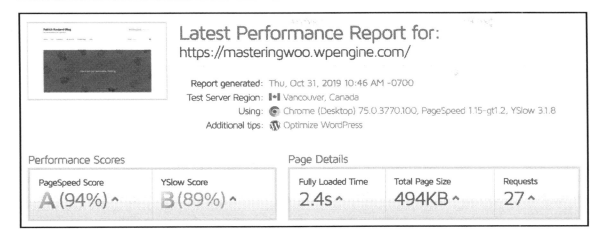

Our performance scores went up and the page details went down.

The **Fully Loaded Time** went from **3.1** to **2.4** seconds.

The **Total Page Size** went from **512** to **494 KB**.

Keep in mind, we're using the exact same HTML, CSS, and JavaScript. They're just served in a different format that's more efficient.

Adding new functionality

Autoptimize and similar plugins minimize and concatenate files. Concatenation is where you combine multiple similar files together. So instead of the browser loading 12 CSS files, there's one concatenated bigger CSS file to download. This saves time and makes your site load faster.

The downside of concatenation is that if you add new functionality it won't automatically be added to the concatenated files; thus, you'll have one CSS file with all of your old functionality and one new CSS file for your new functionality.

To fix this, you need to do one thing after you install a new theme or plugin:

1. Go to **Settings** | **Autoptimize**.
2. Click on **Save Changes and empty cache**.

And any cached files will be recreated the next time someone visits your site.

Now that we've minimized our HTML, CSS, and JavaScript files, it's time to optimize some of the bigger files our site loads: images.

Optimizing images

In the e-commerce world, it's very common to hear that you need high-quality photography to highlight your products. And that's definitely true. You do need good imagery. However, you can't just upload a 2 MB photo to your website. You need to optimize it so it's as small as can be while still being high-quality.

This reduces the total size of a page when someone views your product page. This will make your product page load much faster.

We're going to look into two tools to help us do that: Jetpack and Imagify. First up, we're going to optimize images with Jetpack.

Optimizing images with Jetpack

One of the more well-known tools, and also one that happens to be free, is Jetpack. We already installed Jetpack earlier in this book so it will be pretty easy for us to configure it. Perform the following steps:

1. In WordPress admin, click on **Jetpack** as shown in the following screenshot:

2. Scroll down that page, and you should see a list of Jetpack features. Many of which are disabled by default. Enable **Image Accelerator** (formerly called Photon) as shown in the following screenshot:

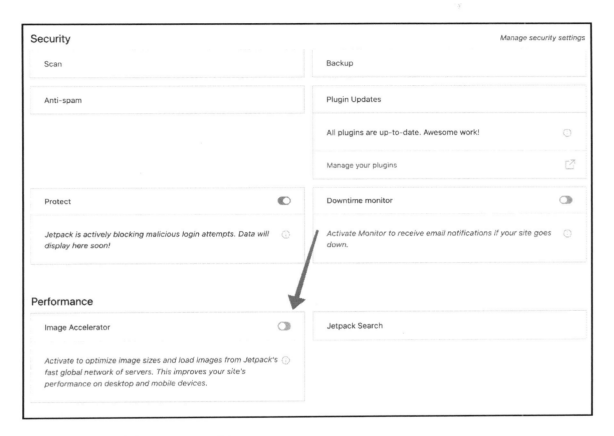

This will do the following two things:

- Image Accelerator will compress images. So that 25 MB photo might only be 400 KB instead.
- It also stores images on WordPress.com servers, and automatically sends images from the closest server.

Both of these help speed up your site, and all we did was toggle one setting.

If you want to test this, then perform the following steps:

1. Go to the frontend of your site and load a product page. It will look as shown in the following screenshot:

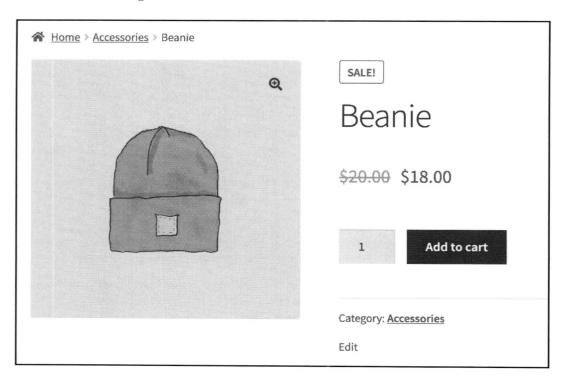

2. View the source of the page. In Google Chrome, you can do this via **View | Developer | View Source**.

And you'll see the code that includes references to WordPress (i0.wp.com). The code is as follows:

```
<a
href="https://i0.wp.com/masteringwoo.wpengine.com/wp-content/upload
s/2019/10/beanie.jpg?fit=801%2C801&amp;ssl=1">
<img width="416" height="416"
src="https://i0.wp.com/masteringwoo.wpengine.com/wp-content/uploads
/2019/10/beanie.jpg?fit=416%2C416&amp;amp;ssl=1" class="wp-post-
image" alt="" title="Beanie" data-caption="" data-
src="https://i0.wp.com/masteringwoo.wpengine.com/wp-content/uploads
/2019/10/beanie.jpg?fit=801%2C801&amp;ssl=1" data-
large_image="https://i0.wp.com/masteringwoo.wpengine.com/wp-content
```

```
/uploads/2019/10/beanie.jpg?fit=801%2C801&amp;ssl=1" data-
large_image_width="801" data-large_image_height="801"
srcset="https://i0.wp.com/masteringwoo.wpengine.com/wp-content/uplo
ads/2019/10/beanie.jpg?w=801&amp;amp;ssl=1 801w,
https://i0.wp.com/masteringwoo.wpengine.com/wp-content/uploads/2019
/10/beanie.jpg?resize=150%2C150&amp;amp;ssl=1 150w,
https://i0.wp.com/masteringwoo.wpengine.com/wp-content/uploads/2019
/10/beanie.jpg?resize=300%2C300&amp;amp;ssl=1 300w,
https://i0.wp.com/masteringwoo.wpengine.com/wp-content/uploads/2019
/10/beanie.jpg?resize=768%2C768&amp;amp;ssl=1 768w" sizes="(max-
width: 416px) 100vw, 416px" />
</a>
```

Our images are now being loaded through `WordPress.com,` and they automatically serve minimized images that speed up our site.

Optimizing images with Imagify

Another tool you could use is Imagify (`https://imagify.io`). This is similar to Jetpack, which compresses and loads your images on its servers to speed up your site. But there are three notable differences:

- They have a free plan and paid plans. You can upload up to 25 MB of photos a month for free, and they'll do everything you need.
- They have more granular control over compression. You can choose by exactly how much you want to compress your images.
- They have a Back button. You can revert changes at any time and recompress your images.

Let's set this up on our site. Perform the following steps:

1. In WordPress admin, go to **Plugins** and click **Add New.**
2. Search for Imagify and click on **Install Now**:

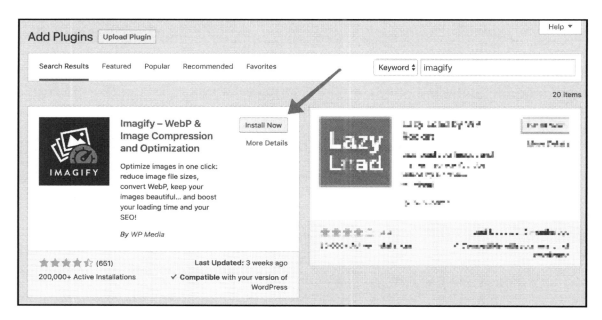

3. Activate the plugin.

4. Now we have to connect to Imagify. Start by creating an account if you haven't done so already:

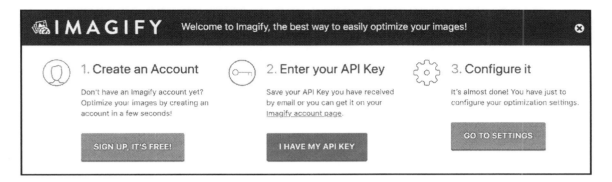

5. Once you've created your account, you should get an email with your API key, and you can also find it through Imagify's site. Click on **I HAVE MY API KEY,** and enter it.

And with that, you're done. Images will automatically be optimized, and you'll make your site quite a bit faster. There's also a handy bulk updater we can use.

Using the bulk updater

Optimizing images one by one is great. But sometimes you need to optimize existing content. That's when you want to have a bulk updater that can do all of this in a few quick and easy steps.

One notable feature that Imagify has is its bulk updater. Let's take a quick tour of that. Perform the following steps:

1. In WordPress admin, click on **Media** and then **Library** as shown in the image below:

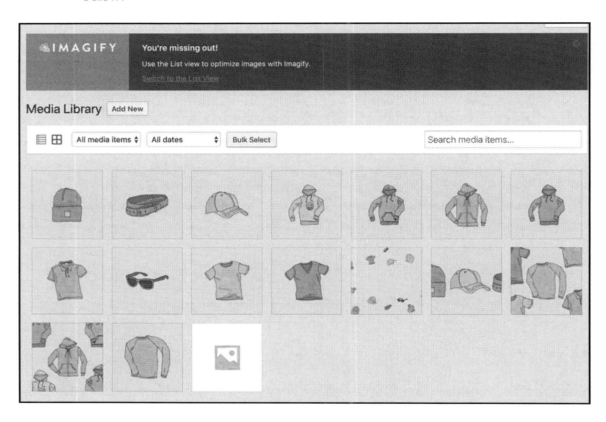

2. You'll see all of your products in a grid. To get the most out of Imagify, click **Switch to the List View** as shown in the previous screenshot.

   From here, we can optimize single images by clicking **Optimize**. Or we can select multiple images and select **Optimize** under **Bulk Actions**:

3. When you're done, you'll see how much you saved by optimizing each image. And it's quite a bit! This can be seen in the following screenshot:

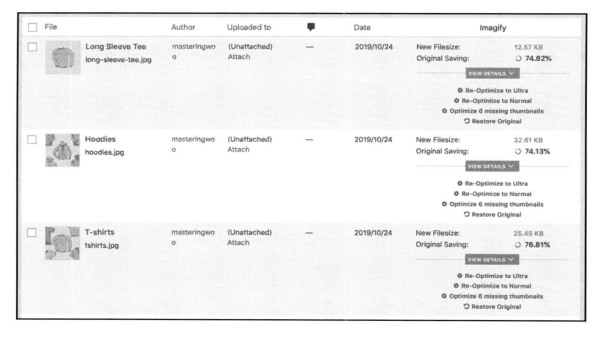

You can do something similar and get into the details through the Imagify menu in the admin bar of your site.

No matter which way you compress your images, your users will thank you for a fast site. Now that we've compressed our images, let's look into caching pages and assets to speed up our site even more.

Caching and e-commerce

Browser caching allows you to speed up your website by storing files locally in the user browser. Essentially, browser caching looks at files you've defined as files that don't change very often and downloads them to the visitor's browser just once. So the next time a visitor visits your home page, they'll already have certain files such as a logo, your style sheet, and credit card icons in the footer of your site.

This doesn't help the very first page someone visits, but it will help with each future page they visit on the site. We're going to configure a caching plugin and discuss page caching and when you'd want to use it.

Configuring caching plugins

Let's take advantage of some browser caching. To configure browser caching plugins, perform the following steps:

1. In your admin under **Add Plugins**, search for WP Fastest Cache and click on **Install Now:**

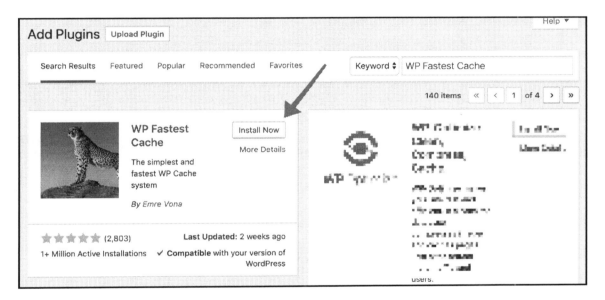

2. Install and activate the plugin.

3. In your main menu, click on **WP Fastest Cache.**
4. Check the checkbox for **Browser Caching** as shown in the following screenshot:

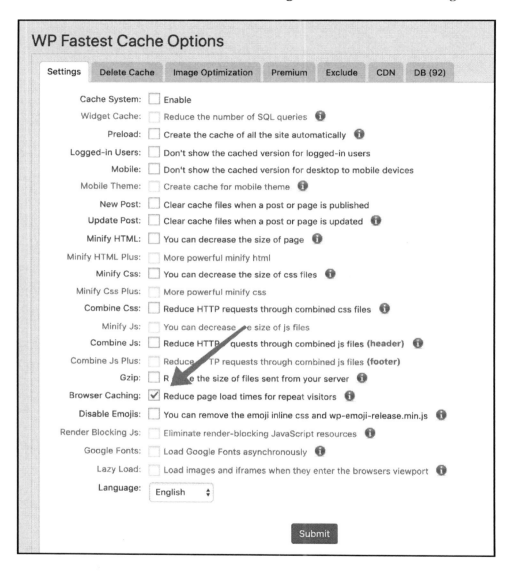

5. Click **Submit** to save your changes.

Configuring caching via HTACCESS

You can also do this through your .htaccess file if you host your site on an Apache server. You'll need to locate your .htaccess file on your server.

Note that with most FTP programs the .htaccess file is hidden so you'll need to enable the option to see hidden files.

Then open that file and add the following code to it:

```
## EXPIRES CACHING ##
<IfModule mod_expires.c>
ExpiresActive On
ExpiresByType image/jpg "access plus 1 month"
ExpiresByType image/jpeg "access plus 1 month"
ExpiresByType image/gif "access plus 1 month"
ExpiresByType image/png "access plus 1 month"
ExpiresByType text/css "access plus 1 month"
ExpiresByType application/pdf "access plus 1 month"
ExpiresByType text/x-javascript "access plus 1 month"
ExpiresByType application/x-shockwave-flash "access plus 1 month"
ExpiresByType image/x-icon "access plus 1 year"
ExpiresDefault "access plus 2 days"
</IfModule>
## EXPIRES CACHING ##
```

If you have the technical expertise, it's a little more efficient to enable this type of caching through .htaccess instead of through a plugin, but of course a plugin is much easier for anyone to install and configure.

Page caching

One thing you should be aware of is the difference between page caching and browser caching. Page caching is where the WordPress site assembles a page (header, main content, images, sidebar, footer, and so on) and saves that page. The next time someone visits that page, the server provides the cached page.

This works great for static sites, such as news sites. But with e-commerce there are pages you can't cache, such as the cart and checkout. And there are elements within other pages you don't want to cache, such as the cart icon (which usually shows how many items are in your cart) and related products.

Page caching has some big problems with e-commerce. You can attempt to cache some pages, but it's often more trouble than it's worth.

WooCommerce has a list of compatible caching plugins (`https://docs.woocommerce.com/document/configuring-caching-plugins/`) and any modifications you need to make.

Now that we know how to cache our content, we can optimize the content above the fold.

Optimizing content above the fold

On a typical product page, there are a half dozen images. And many of them are "below the fold." The fold is a term from the newspaper industry where there was a literal fold. You wanted your best headlines and photos to be above the fold so everyone would see them.

In the following screenshot, you can see where my fold is on my laptop and what is considered above and below the fold:

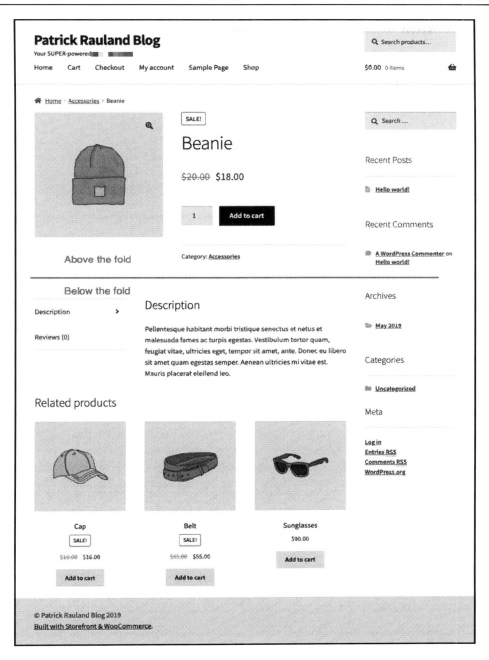

In the web world, we still use the fold terminology but we talk about it in different ways. And when it comes to optimization we can "lazy-load" our images. Lazy loading means we only download the image once the viewer starts scrolling down.

A few of the plugins we've looked at in this chapter will do this for us. But I want to show you how to do this with a free plugin that we've already installed.

Lazy loading images with Jetpack

In WordPress admin, we can enable lazy loading. Perform the following steps:

1. Click on **Jetpack** in your admin.
2. Click on **Settings** under Jetpack.
3. Check the box for **Enable Lazy Loading for images** as shown in the following screenshot:

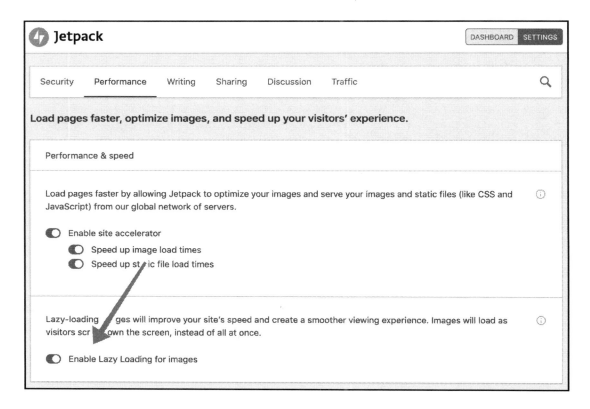

Jetpack should automatically save the setting immediately.

That's all we have to do for this one. This helps our users and all you have to do is tick a checkbox.

Summary

Optimizing a site can be a full-time job. There are plenty of WordPress developers who do this for 40 hours a week, and if you really want to optimize your site you can get a 100% score on GTMetrix.

But if you only want to spend an hour or two optimizing your site, you can still make huge gains and improvements. If you followed all of the advice in this chapter, you should have seen a pretty big speed improvement through GTMetrix.

In this chapter, you have learned how to monitor performance with GTMetrix, minify static files such as CSS and JavaScript, optimize images, cache certain parts of your site, and optimize content above the fold by lazy-loading images.

In the next chapter, we're going to configure our theme.

10
Setting Up Your Theme

Up until this point, we've focused on what your store can do. But just as important as what your store can do is how your store looks. Do you want a busy look or a clean and minimalist look? Each will cater to a different audience.

In this chapter, we're going to look into how you can control the important visual aspects of your store. We'll dig into the following:

- Choosing a theme for WooCommerce
- Rearranging the product page
- Adding a product data tab

By the end of this chapter, you should know how to choose a theme build for WooCommerce, customize the appearance of your store so that your store reflects your brand, add a product tab, and install a plugin to see the frontend hooks.

The first thing we're going to look into is choosing a theme for an online store.

Choosing a theme for WooCommerce

There are thousands of themes on WordPress.org. But not all of these themes are going to work well with WooCommerce. Many of them are designed for brochure websites or blogs. We want a theme that has space for lots of products and lots of space on the product page for all sorts of information.

We're going to take a look into some of the most popular themes for WooCommerce, including the following:

- Twenty Twenty
- Storefront
- Astra

We're going to look into how to set up each of these themes and the benefits of each one. First up is Twenty Twenty.

Exploring the Twenty Twenty theme

Twenty Twenty is the most recent version of the default theme released with WordPress. Each year, WordPress releases a new default theme and the current version is Twenty Twenty (`https://wordpress.org/themes/twentytwenty/`). All of these themes are available for free and they're a great place to start any WordPress project.

One of the best features of the default themes is they almost always show off the new features built into WordPress. Since Gutenberg blocks were such a focus in WordPress for the last year, the Twenty Twenty theme really takes those blocks and makes them look great.

Let's take a look at a real blog post using those new blocks. Follow these steps:

1. Log in to your WordPress admin.
2. Navigate to **Appearance** | **Themes** and you should see Twenty Twenty in your list of themes, as we can see in the following screenshot:

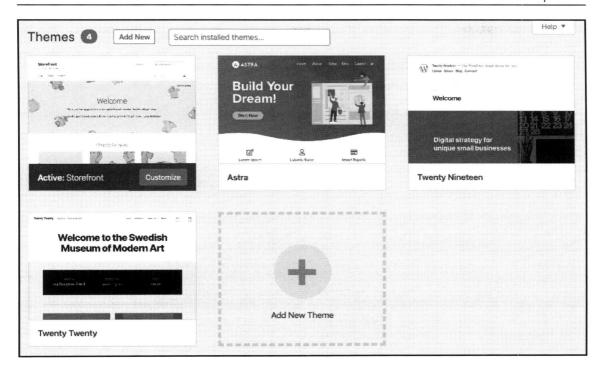

If you don't see Twenty Twenty, then click **Add New Theme** and search for
Twenty Twenty to find and install it.

3. Hover over **Twenty Twenty** and click **Activate**.

The theme is now activated. Let's take a look around the theme.

If you browse to the **Shop** page, you'll see a pretty bare page. My shop can be seen in the following screenshot:

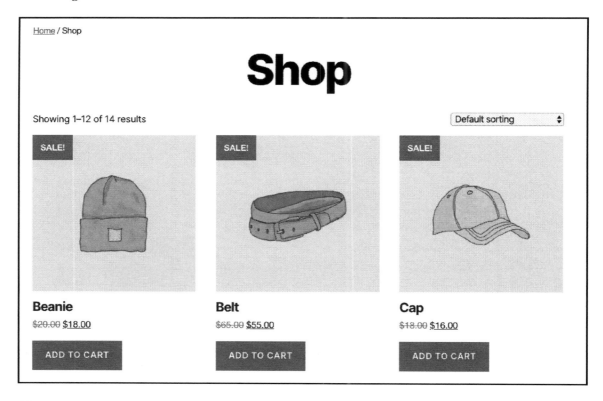

The store page is a bit bare. You can easily change the colors through the WordPress customizer but you're likely going to want to have a bit more color and other graphical elements.

Now let's take a look at a page that uses those blocks. Follow these steps:

1. In your WordPress admin, click on **Pages**.
2. Find your home page (usually called **Home**).
3. Add or customize the existing blocks.
4. I recommend using the **Cover**, **Best Selling Products**, **Featured Product**, and **On Sale Products** blocks.

5. When you're adding or editing blocks, I also recommend using the **Wide** width orientation or **Full** width, which you can see in the following:

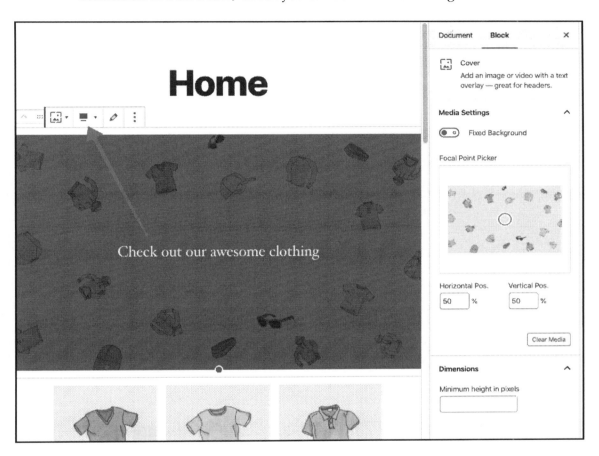

6. Save the page.

Once you've added blocks, using the full width or wide width setting, take a look at the frontend. Here's my very simple home page with four blocks using those settings:

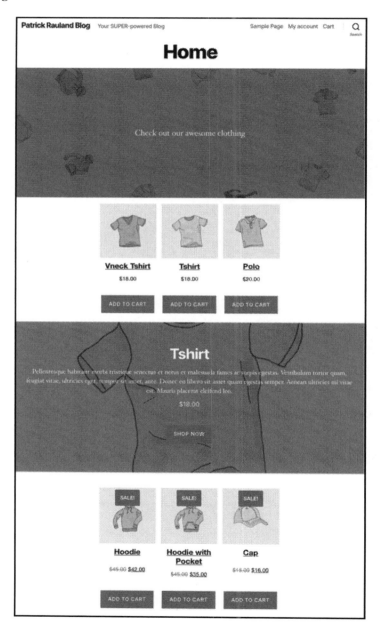

Because the theme is so empty, it's perfect for customizing with blocks. If you want to build very customized pages with blocks, then this theme could be a great fit for you.

If you have a more standard e-commerce site and you don't expect to be making tons of custom pages like this, then you might want to check out Storefront and Astra.

Storefront

One of my favorite themes to recommend is Storefront (`https://woocommerce.com/storefront/`). It's a free theme and it's built by the WooCommerce team. It's the theme they use to test every feature against, so if you want the most reliable theme or the theme where you know every piece of WooCommerce functionality will look great, then you'll want to check out Storefront.

You may have already installed and activated Storefront going through the WooCommerce welcome wizard.

If you haven't, you can install it by following these steps:

1. Go to your WordPress admin.
2. Go to **Appearance** | **Themes**.
3. Clicking **Add New Theme**.
4. Search for `Storefront` and install.

Storefront has a few things going for it. The first is that it includes these nice product images we've seen in this book. If you want to set up a test store, you can use Storefront just for the nice test products they import. But there's a lot more to Storefront including product page functionality that's built in.

We're going to look into the following:

- The sticky add-to-cart button
- Paginating between products

Sticky add-to-cart button

One of the most useful features that's included with Storefront is a sticky add-to-cart button. When you're looking at a product page, you'll see the **Add to cart** button in its usual place. This can be seen in the following screenshot:

When you start strolling down, as soon as you scroll past the add-to-cart button, it should be added to a sticky bar at the top of the page. Here's what it looks like on my laptop:

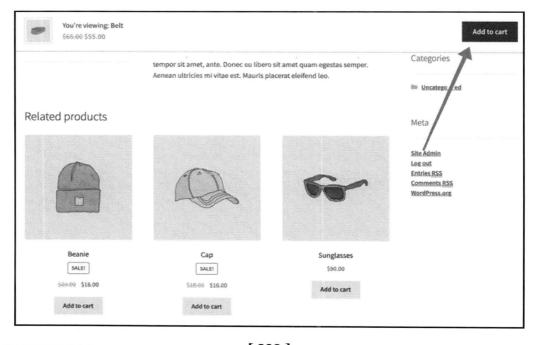

This functionality is built into Storefront. You can disable it by following these steps:

1. Navigate to the WordPress customizer.
2. Click into the **Product Page** settings.
3. Disable the setting for **Sticky Add-To-Cart**, which you can see here:

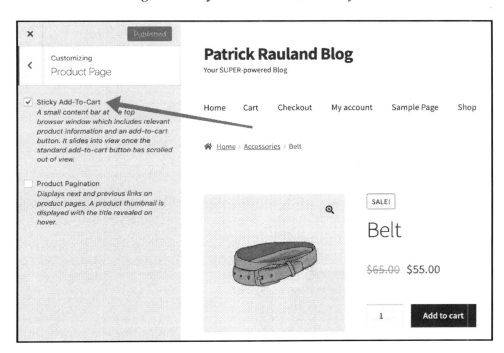

4. Click **Publish** to save your changes.

If for some reason this functionality is turned off by default, you can turn it on on the same setting page. I am a big fan of this setting since it really helps users as they scroll down the page.

Product pagination

Pagination lets you navigate between different areas of the site. While we're on this settings page, let's enable product pagination. This lets us navigate between different products.

You can see what it looks like on my site:

In addition, as you hover over the images, they slide out and give you the product title.

I'm happy they included this functionality in this theme but for my own purposes, I find it clutters up the product page and navigating through products this way seems a little tedious and unintuitive. Still, if you like this functionality, go for it. It's great to have it built into the theme instead of having to install a bunch of plugins.

Exploring Astra

There's one final theme that is worth mentioning. This time because it's free and fast. Astra is a very tiny theme and it's designed to load quickly (`https://wordpress.org/themes/astra/`). If you're a fan of speed and lightning-fast pages, then Astra will help you to get there (in addition to the previous chapter).

Here's the GTMetrix report of our site with Storefront:

Here's the same report after switching to Astra:

The total page size decreased and the fully loaded time dropped 0.7 seconds and its now below the target 2 second load time.

This theme doesn't have many options and, for store owners who value speed, this is hugely helpful.

If you like the idea of a fast theme, you can get Astra for free or you can check out the Pro version of Astra, which has additional features and customization options.

All of the themes we've covered in this section are good at certain things and not great in other areas. It's totally up to you and what's important for your brand when you pick a theme.

Next up, let's look at how we can view hook on the front of our site so we can customize our theme further.

Viewing hooks on the Frontend

It's very common for store owners to want to customize the frontend of their store. They might really like the look of the product page but they want to rearrange certain elements.

In this section, we're going to install a plugin to help us to understand how the WooCommerce code works so that we can modify it.

As an example, let's say we take a look at our product page and we don't think listing the category is important for our store. We could move that lower down the page. But how would we even begin to do that?

In the following screenshot, how do we move **Category: Tshirts** lower down the page? Take a look:

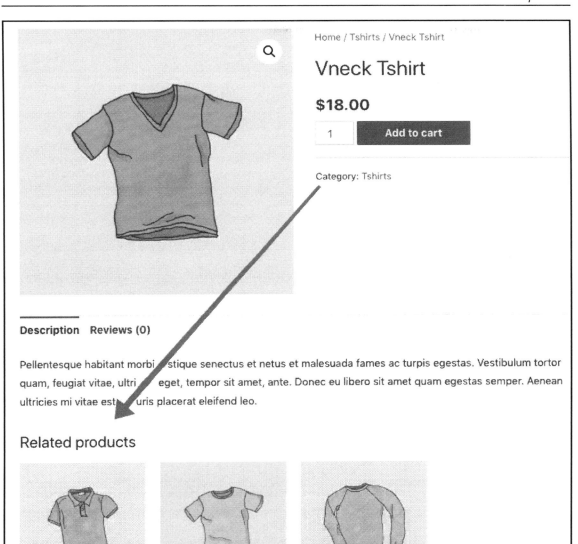

The answer is simple: the first thing we have to do is find where this code is coming from and how it's being displayed on the page. We could go through thousands of lines of code in WooCommerce or we could use what I call hook visualizer tools, which we will be looking at in the next section.

Installing hook visualizers

Hook visualizers are tools made for developers. They help you to know exactly what code is running when. Let's install one and you'll see how useful they can be. Follow these steps:

1. In your WordPress admin, go to **Plugins** | **Add New**.
2. Search for `Simply Show Hooks`:

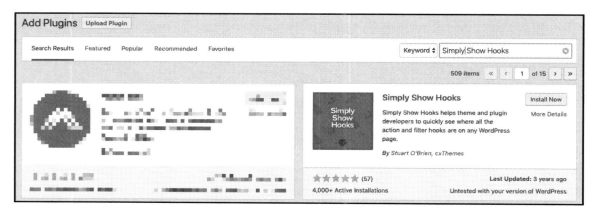

3. Install and activate the plugin.

4. Go to the frontend of your site and you'll see a new menu:

5. Hover over **Simply Show Hooks** and click **Show Action Hooks**. This will make the page reload with a ton of extra data, which we can see in the following:

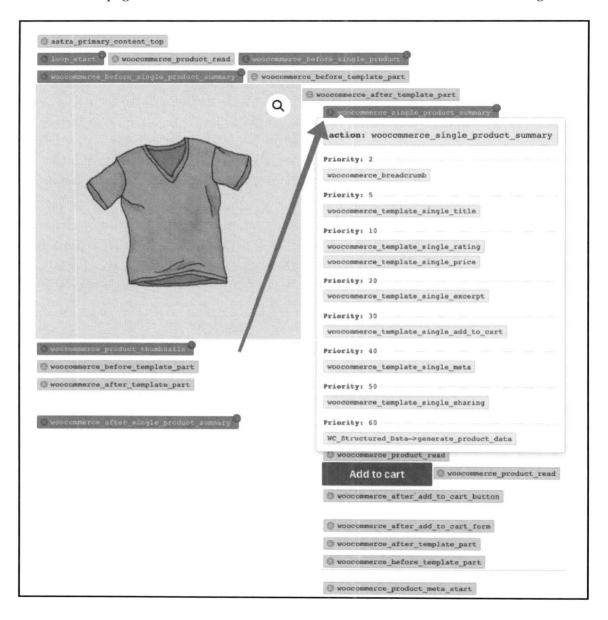

Here, you can see every action. Actions in WordPress are where code is executed. Under `woocommerce_single_product_summary`, you can see there are nine separate pieces of functionality. We can see the priority for each of them, which is the order they come out in.

Once we know this information, we can write code to change that priority.

If you're familiar with WordPress actions (`https://developer.wordpress.org/plugins/hooks/actions/`), you can unhook any code and write new code to hook it in in a new place. This isn't a book about the WordPress action system, so we can't go into too much detail here. But this is the real power of WooCommerce. With the WordPress action system, you can remove or add anything you want.

Stop showing hooks

The Simply Show Hooks plugin only shows hooks to the admin of the site. So, your users won't see these. However, they still take up a lot of space. At any point, you can hover over **Simply Show Hooks** and click **Stop Showing Action Hooks**.

Browsing through code for actions

I'm a huge fan of hook visualizers because you can navigate to a page and see the actions on that page and then reverse engineer what you have to do. But sometimes, you don't even know where to start. In that case, it's helpful to be familiar with the code base.

WooCommerce has a helpful beginner guide to actions (`https://docs.woocommerce.com/document/introduction-to-hooks-actions-and-filters/`). More importantly, they have a complete hook reference (`https://docs.woocommerce.com/wc-apidocs/hook-docs.html`). You can browse through this resource and find any hook and read more about it.

As an example, I can search for `woocommerce_single_product_summary`. This can be seen in the following screenshot:

woocommerce_sidebar	action	archive-product.php, single-product.php
woocommerce_single_product_image_gallery_classes	filter	product-image.php
woocommerce_single_product_image_thumbnail_html	filter	product-image.php, product-thumbnails.php
woocommerce_single_product_summary	action	content-single-product.php
woocommerce_terms_is_checked_default	filter	terms.php

I can click `woocommerce_single_product_summary` and I will be taken to the exact code that controls this functionality. We can see that in the following screenshot:

```
46        <div class="summary entry-summary">
47            <?php
48            /**
49             * Hook: woocommerce_single_product_summary.
50             *
51             * @hooked woocommerce_template_single_title - 5
52             * @hooked woocommerce_template_single_rating - 10
53             * @hooked woocommerce_template_single_price - 10
54             * @hooked woocommerce_template_single_excerpt - 20
55             * @hooked woocommerce_template_single_add_to_cart - 30
56             * @hooked woocommerce_template_single_meta - 40
57             * @hooked woocommerce_template_single_sharing - 50
58             * @hooked WC_Structured_Data::generate_product_data() - 60
59             */
60            do_action( 'woocommerce_single_product_summary' );
61            ?>
62        </div>
63
```

If you are comfortable with code, then browsing through the code might be the best option for you. But for most of us, I recommend starting with a hook visualizer tool. We can see most of what we need with that tool.

Let's look into how to add a product data tab.

Adding a product data tab

WooCommerce has a nice tab system on the product page. It's the perfect place to add custom information to your product. If you have extra information you really want to share with your audience rather than burying it in the product description, you can add it to a custom tab.

This can be done with code but there are also several easy to use plugins. We're going to use Custom Product Tabs for WooCommerce since it's free. But there are more powerful paid plugins available.

We're going to install a custom tab plugin and then configure that plugin.

Installing a custom tab plugin

Let's start by installing the right plugin. Follow these steps:

1. In your WordPress admin, go to **Plugins | Add New**.
2. Search for **Custom Product Tabs for WooCommerce** as seen here:

3. Install and activate the plugin.

Adding a custom tab

Now that we have the plugin installed, we can add a custom tab to a page. Follow these steps:

1. In your WordPress admin, edit one of your products.
2. If you scroll down to the **Product data** panel, you'll see an extra tab called **Custom Tabs**, as seen here:

3. Click **Add a Tab**.
4. Add a title and description for the tab, as shown here:

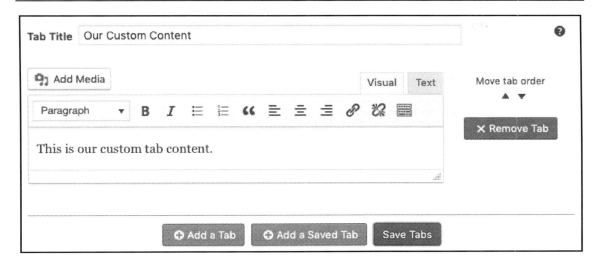

5. Click **Save Tabs.**

6. Click **Update** to finish updating the product.

Now, if you take a look at the frontend, you'll see our custom tab and content:

This is only the start of custom tabs. You can add additional tabs, and you can even save tabs and then apply them to multiple or even all of your product pages. This is really helpful for some information, such as sizing charts.

Summary

Customizing the frontend of your store is important. It's what people see and remember, and there are lots of ways to do it. By now you should be familiar with three of the most popular themes for WooCommerce and you hopefully installed one of these themes. You also know how to look at the front of your site with a hook visualizer so you can see where certain code actions are taking place. And with plugins, you can customize the tabs that appear on the product pages. You now know how to customize your own store after reading this chapter.

We're going to look into customizing specific parts of the product page in the next chapter with functionality you might not have considered.

Customizing the Product Page

11

We've set up our theme. Now, it's time to add more information to our product page in order to make it enticing, and so that more users are inclined to buy our products.

We're going to add social proof and a few different types of media to the product page. Social proof shows users that other people are actively using and purchasing products on this site, which makes users feel safe, and adding extra media such as videos or 360-degree images will give the user more context to help them determine whether this is the right product for them.

The following topics will be covered in this chapter:

- Adding social proof
- Adding a video tab to the product page
- Adding 360-degree images

By the end of this chapter, you should know how to make your product page a lot more informative and visually interesting.

Adding social proof (FOMO)

Human beings are social creatures. If we see another person doing something, then we assume that it's okay for us to do that same thing. That's why, when we see a whole group of people gathering, we want to see what they're gathering around. We call this behavior social proof. And it's something that we can also add to our website.

There are lots of types of social proof, including the following:

- Product reviews
- Followers on social media

But in this section, we're going to talk about seeing other people doing the thing that you want them to do. If you visit Fomo website (`https://fomo.com`), you'll see activity at the bottom of the site. You can see this in the following image:

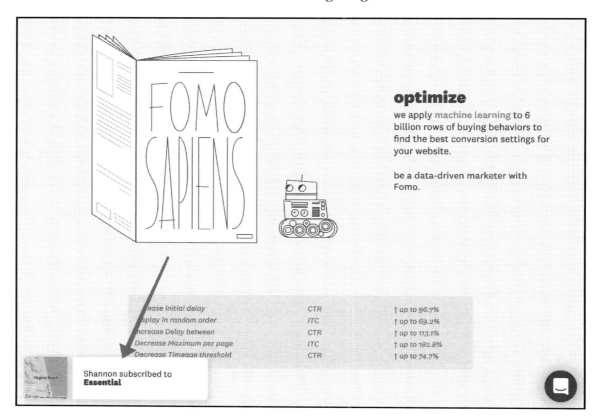

We can see that a real user was active on the site. That makes it much more likely for me to do that same activity.

We're going to set that up on our e-commerce site, so that anytime someone purchases a product, we broadcast that to other users in order to make them more likely to do the same activity.

We're going to set up FOMO and customize the notifications.

Setting up FOMO

The first step is to go to `https://fomo.com` and create an account. Once you have done that, you can connect it to your store. Follow these steps to set up FOMO:

1. Log in to your FOMO account.
2. Add your first store, by adding your store's URL, as shown in the following image:

3. Next, choose the appearance of the notification:

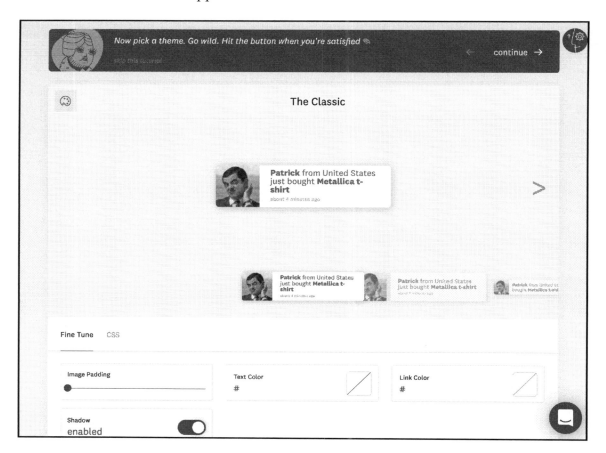

 You can change this later. So feel free to choose a style, continue setting up FOMO, and then come back later to make sure that all of the details are correct.

4. Now, we have to connect FOMO to our WooCommerce store. We can do that with the WooCommerce API. Skip to the end of the wizard.

5. Within WooCommerce, navigate to **WooCommerce** | **Settings** | **Advanced** | **REST API**.

6. Click **Create API Key**, as shown in the following screenshot:

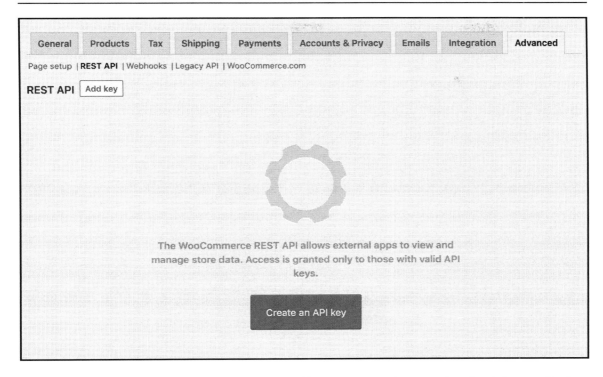

7. Call the key FOMO and give it read/write permissions under the **Advanced** tab, as shown in the following screenshot:

8. Click **Generate API key**.
9. Within FOMO, navigate to **Integrations** and copy and paste the **Consumer Key** and **Consumer Secret** from WooCommerce to FOMO, as shown in the following screenshot:

Lastly, we need to add the FOMO JavaScript code to our site. There are a couple of ways to do this. These are as follows:

- We could add the JavaScript code directly to our theme files. If we custom created our own theme or child theme, we could take this route.
- We could add the JavaScript code through a plugin. This is a bit easier, and anyone can do it.

Let's add that JavaScript code. Perform the following steps:

1. In your WordPress admin, install and activate the Insert Headers and Footers plugin (`https://wordpress.org/plugins/insert-headers-and-footers/`).
2. Within FOMO, navigating the **copy to clipboard** button, which is shown in the following screenshot:

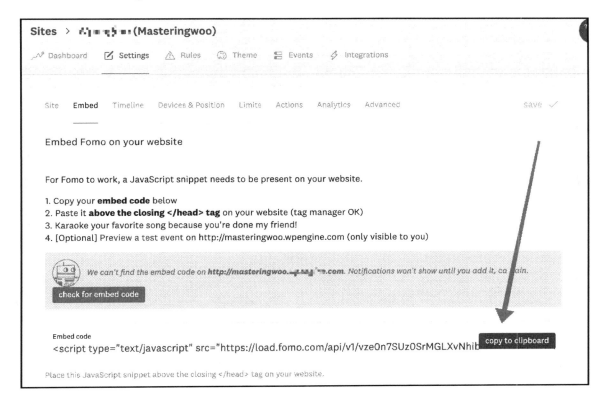

3. Navigate to **Settings | Insert Headers and Footers** and paste the JavaScript code into the footer box, as shown in the following screenshot:

4. Save.
5. Go back to FOMO and click **check for embed code**.
6. It takes a few minutes, but you should see a success message that the code is appearing on your site:

7. Click **Preview a test event**, and you should see a test event:

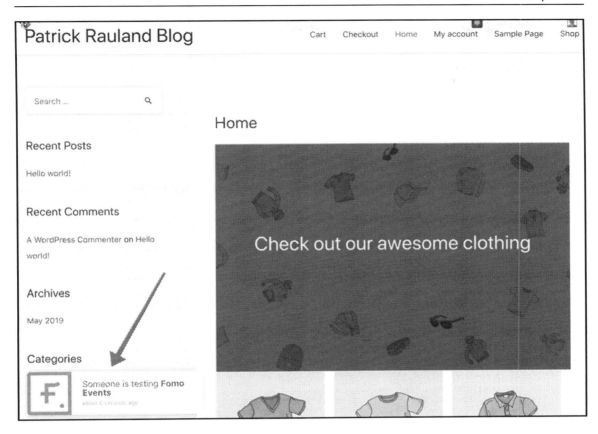

And with that, we have set up FOMO. FOMO is automatically going to record important events, such as users purchasing products, and then display them on the frontend.

Now, we can customize what the notifications look like.

Customizing notifications

For the most part, FOMO is going to automatically pull in useful notifications and display them on your site. However, you can always customize what you see. If you want to show really big product photos, you can do that, or you can highlight where in the world your customers are purchasing from, or you can keep it really minimal and just say that someone purchased a product.

In the end, it's totally up to you, and you can customize your notifications to make your brand.

Removing events

If you've been testing products, orders, payments, and suchlike on your site, then you might have some test data that you want to clear up.

In FOMO, you can click on **Events** and you can see all of the events that FOMO picked up, and if you hover over one of them, you'll see a **remove** popup. You can click this to remove any invalid or test data.

In the following screenshot, **Bob in Venture** is actually the test data that I need to remove:

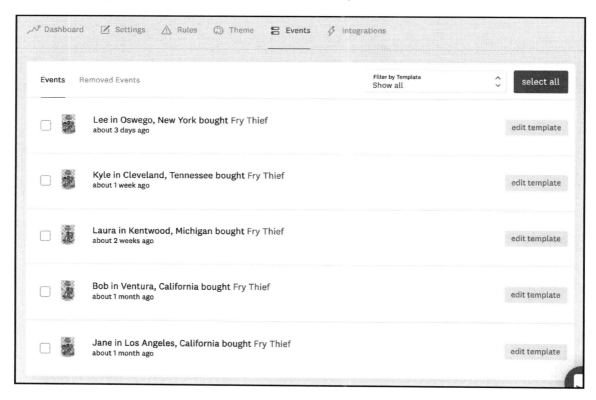

Once we've removed any incorrect data, we can customize on what devices these notifications are displayed.

Hiding notifications on mobile

Sometimes, notifications like these sound great, but when you're on a tiny device, they might actually prevent you from viewing the site entirely.

If you want to give your users a better mobile experience, you can disable FOMO on mobile devices.

Perform the following steps:

1. In FOMO, navigate to **Settings** | **Devices & Position**.

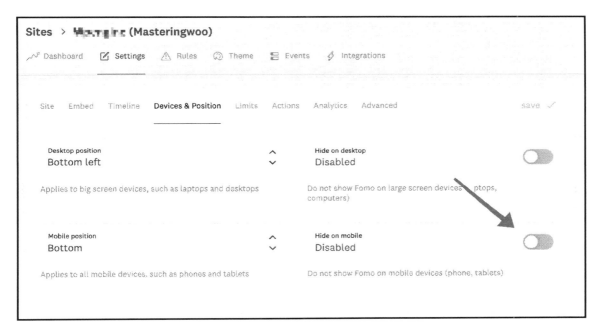

2. Enable the radio button to **Hide on mobile**, as shown in the preceding screenshot.
3. Click **Save**.

FOMO will now only display on tablets and on desktop devices. It won't display on mobile devices.

Customizing notification frequency

You might also want to choose how often these notifications appear. On busy stores, you might want to show a notification every 2 seconds. But on a smaller, more niche store, maybe you only want to show a notification every 12 seconds.

As an example, I might only want to show notifications to users who have been on my site for 10 seconds or more.

To do so, perform the following steps:

1. In FOMO, navigate to **Settings | Timeline.**
2. Change Initial delay (seconds) from 6 to 10, as shown in the previous screenshot.
3. Click **Save.**

As you can see, FOMO is pretty much a set-it-and-forget-it technology. There isn't much management, and it shows new visitors to your store what other people are actually looking at and buying.

Now that users know that other people are actively buying products on our store, let's look at providing users with video information on the product page.

Adding a video tab

People like to consume information in a variety of ways. Some people like reading text and images, others like word of mouth and talking about a product, and others still prefer a video that's fully engaging for a few minutes and describes the product in detail. Most of us like some combination of these at different times for different products.

In this section, we're going to add a video tab to our product page so that there's a designated place for it.

We're going to start by installing the video tab and then move on to customizing it.

Installing a video tab

There are a number of plugins that let you add videos to your WooCommerce page, many of which are free. We're going to use WooCommerce HTML5 Video (`https://wordpress.org/plugins/woocommerce-html5-video/`). Perform the following steps:

1. In your WordPress admin, go to **Plugins | Add New** and search for `WooCommerce HTML5 Video`.
2. Install and activate the plugin.

And that's all we need for installing—pretty fast and easy.

Configuring a video with WooCommerce

The plugin that we just installed allows you to load HTML5 video natively. This means that you upload the movie to your server, and the users download it directly from you. That certainly works, but it is a lot more work for the average store owner.

What I generally recommend is to use video hosting, such as YouTube or Vimeo. Their servers are already designed to serve videos quickly and efficiently.

Before we get started, find a YouTube or Vimeo video. Follow the next steps to add your own video to your product page.

1. In the backend of your WooCommerce site, edit a product.
2. As you scroll down to the **Product data** panel, you'll see something like what is shown in the following screenshot. You can add a bit of text with a rich text editor, and then add videos:

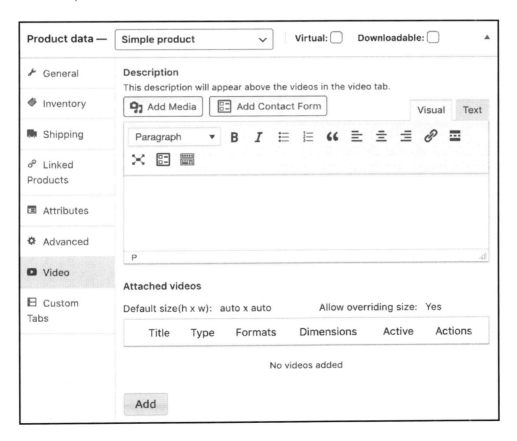

3. Click **Add** and you'll see a new popup, which can be seen in the following screenshot:

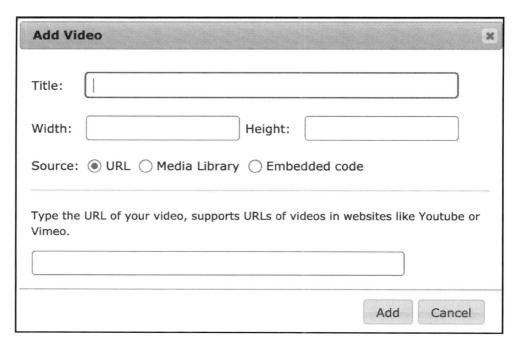

4. Add the URL of your video.
5. You have the option to add height, width, and title, although I recommend not adding them, to see if you like the look without adding extra data.
6. Click **Add.**
7. Click **Update** to save your product.

On the frontend of your site, you'll see something similar to the following screenshot:

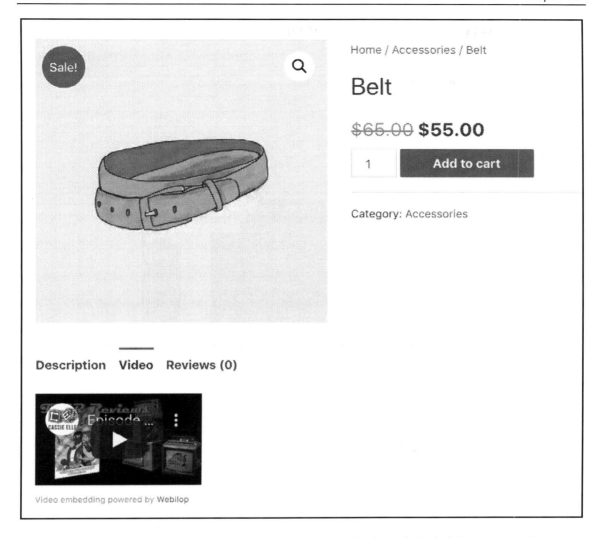

We're now displaying videos for our visitors. This can be hugely helpful in persuading them to actually purchase your products.

Configuring defaults

Oftentimes, all of your videos will look good with the same dimensions. This plugin lets you set defaults for all of your videos. Let's set some defaults, so our videos look a little better. Perform the following steps:

1. In the WordPress admin, navigate to **Settings** | **WooCommerce HTML5 Video**. You'll see something similar to the following screenshot:

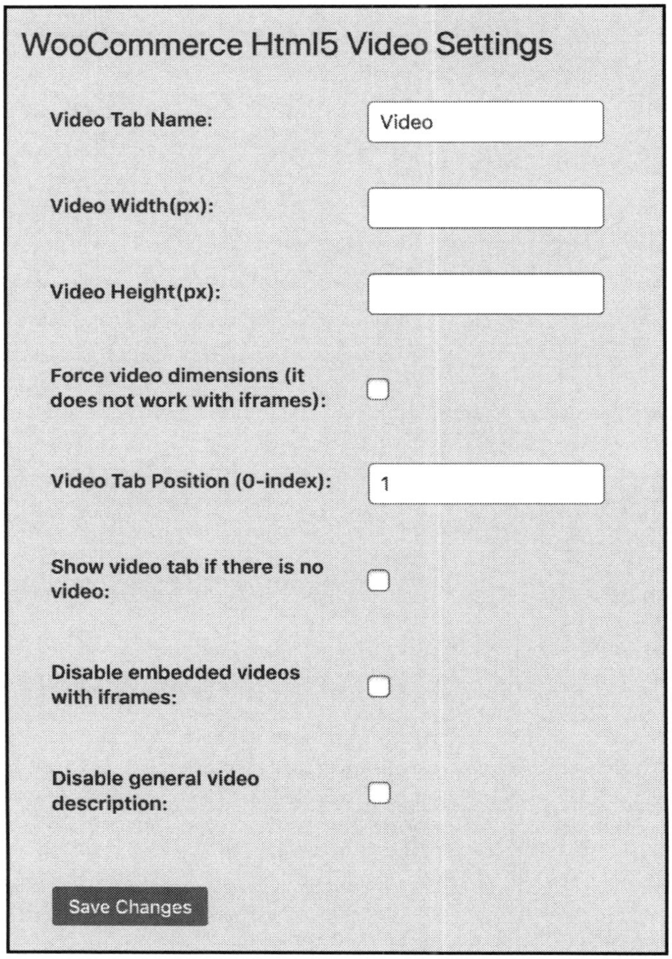

WooCommerce Html5 Video Settings

Video Tab Name: `Video`

Video Width(px): ` `

Video Height(px): ` `

Force video dimensions (it does not work with iframes): ☐

Video Tab Position (0-index): `1`

Show video tab if there is no video: ☐

Disable embedded videos with iframes: ☐

Disable general video description: ☐

Save Changes

2. Add a default width and height in the fields shown in the previous screenshot (I started with a width of 600 and a height of 400), and click **Save**.

My product page can be seen in the following screenshot:

Now, our videos are quite large and no one should overlook them. If video content is important to us, these settings are great.

Hiding the credit

Oftentimes, plugin authors will add a credit in the plugin, and say something to the effect of the *X feature provided by Y*. This plugin does just that. However, you don't always want to have a ton of credits listed all over your site, especially not on your product page.

Refer to the following screenshot for the default credit:

Most plugin authors give you a way to disable these credits, but this plugin doesn't, so we have to write a bit of CSS in order to hide it. Perform the following steps to hide the plugin credits:

1. Navigate to **Appearance | Customize.**
2. Click **Additional CSS**.
3. Add the following CSS:

```
#tab-html5_video p {
display: none;
}
```

4. Click **Publish**.

5. Navigate back to the video page, and you will see that the credits are gone, which can be seen in the following screenshot:

Our products now have videos that clearly explain and highlight them. Giving your users video reviews, testimonials, and overviews of your products can be very helpful to them, and it only takes a few minutes of your time.

Now, we can look into some of the ways of adding images, which cover every aspect of a product.

Displaying 360-degree images

Humans are very visual, and we like to see images alongside a written description. And one image isn't enough. Customers want to see multiple angles. Several well-known online stores (`https://cxl.com/blog/how-images-can-boost-your-conversion-rate/`) have tested this, and they've seen conversions improve by 10-30%. That's why we're going to look into displaying images that cover 360 degrees of a product.

We're going to use WooCommerce 360º Image (`https://woocommerce.com/products/woocommerce-360-image/`) to show off multiple angles of our products. We're going to start by installing the plugin, followed by adding product photos. When we're done, users will be able to see every aspect of our product, and will be much more likely to add the item to their cart and check out.

Installing WooCommerce 360º Image

This is a premium plugin, so if you want to use it, you'll have to purchase it from WooCommerce.com. Perform the following steps:

1. Purchase WooCommerce 360º Image on WooCommerce.com.
2. Download the zip file with the plugin.
3. In your WordPress site, go to **Plugins** | **Add New** and upload the zip file.
4. Activate the plugin after it has finished uploading.

That's all we need from an installation standpoint. Now, to configure it with our products.

If you don't have your own photos, the page for WooCommerce 360º Image links to a zip file, which contains a few example images.

Adding 360 images to products

Let's create a new product, and then add images to that product. Perform the following steps:

1. In the admin, create a new product by clicking on **Products** | **Add New.**
2. Give the product a title, a price, and a description, if you so wish.

3. Check the box for **Replace Image with 360 Image**:

4. Under **Product Gallery**, upload your images, as shown in the following screenshot:

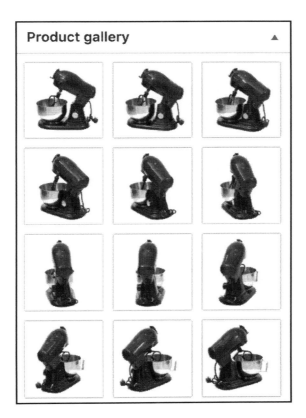

It's easier to get the photos in the correct order if the filenames are sequential (ex. `product_1.jpg`, `product_2.jpg`).

5. Publish your product.

On the frontend, you'll see the 360 image functionality. You can rotate the product left and right. You can also press the play icon and watch the product spin around, as shown in the following screenshot:

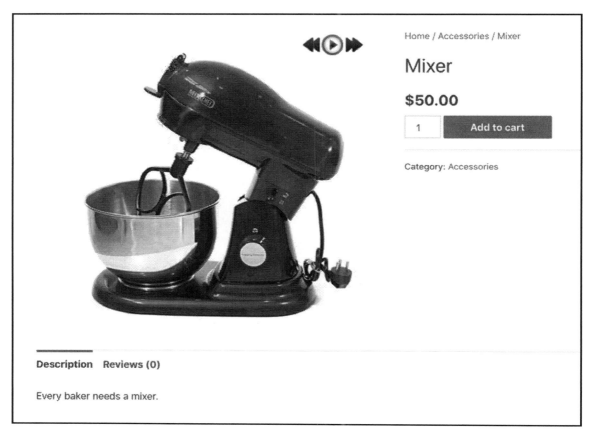

Until we get to the point of shopping through virtual reality, this is the closest thing for store owners. From a technical perspective, it's easy to set up. The hardest part is getting good quality pictures and getting enough photos.

But once you do, the effect is great for your users.

Summary

A default WooCommerce product page is fine. It's done the job, but it doesn't really stand out. The technologies that we covered in this chapter make your product page stand out, and make it more likely that someone will purchase from you.

By now, you should be able to integrate your store with FOMO, and display social proof to new users. You can add a video tab to your product pages and display multiple videos. And you can use a 360-degree image to show multiple angles of a product.

All of these things will make your store more appealing, and they require almost no maintenance or ongoing work.

In the next chapter, we will look at how to build a landing page with WooCommerce Blocks.

12
Building a Landing Page

A common strategy when announcing a new product or service is to create a landing page for that product. These can be used to educate potential customers about the new product or to get sales. They're usually quite in-depth with images, text, headlines, quotes, and sometimes user-submitted content. These all help a potential customer to understand what the product is, and why they would want it. They're also designed so that all of the information is on one page. That way, users don't get lost, and they hopefully sign up with their email or make a purchase. Once you know how to build a landing page, you can build one quickly in order to gauge interest in a potential product before launching, and once you have a product, you can secure sales.

We're going to build a landing page to capture pre-orders for a new product that we're launching. Then, we are going to start by building a regular landing page, after which, we will add e-commerce functionality to the landing page. Finally, we're going to create multiple versions of the landing page and use A/B testing software to figure out which version will lead to better outcomes (email sign-ups or sales).

Throughout this chapter, I'm going to create a landing page for a new board game (Mintsugi), but you can create a landing page for any product.

The following topics will be covered in this chapter:

- Building a long-form landing page
- Adding e-commerce features to a landing page
- A/B test everything

Let's get started by building a landing page.

Building a long-form landing page

Landing pages are typically a special type of page that is used to explain and (hopefully) sell a product or service, and they come in all sorts of formats. Sometimes, they're very short with just an email, a sign-up form, and a photo. We're going to build a long-form landing page for a new product that we're offering.

This longer landing page gives us plenty of space to explain the product, to see customer feedback, and to see photos and videos.

Let's start by creating a page, then we'll structure our page so that we know where to add the content, and finally, we'll add the content to our landing page.

Creating a new page

Before we can build a landing page to sell someone a product, we have to start with the basics by creating a page in WordPress. Let's build a solid foundation before we get into the more technical part.

We can create a new page by following these steps:

1. In your WordPress admin center go to **Pages**.
2. Click on **Add New**, which you can see here:

3. Add a title to our page, which you can see here:

And that's all we *have* to do. There is one optional setting that you can change, which will make a big difference to the landing pages: enabling a full-width template. Landing pages should be focused exclusively on selling the product or the service. You don't want, or need, a sidebar to distract your visitors from other information.

In my Astra theme, I have an option to remove the sidebar. You might find this in a different setting in your theme. You can reach out to your theme developer, or look through their documentation, to see how to do this in the theme. You can see how to do it in Astra, here:

 Many, but not all, themes have an option for removing a sidebar on a page. If you really want to use landing pages, you should look into a theme that supports this option.

Understanding structure of a landing page

To get an idea of what a landing page looks like, let's take a look at one on WooCommerce.com (`https://woocommerce.com`). There's a landing page for store owners (`https://woocommerce.com/store-owners/`) that tells them all about the software. I'm including a screenshot; however, this is maybe one third of the landing page. It's very long and there isn't enough space to show you the whole thing, so I encourage you to visit the page to get the full experience:

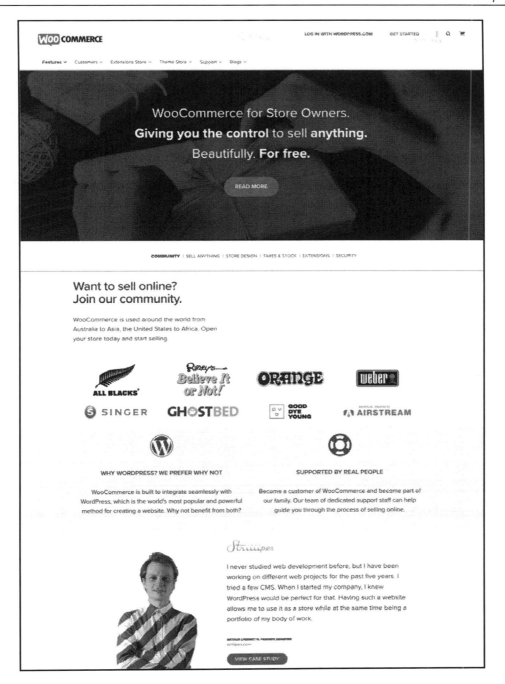

You can see that there are lots of individual sections. They highlight the following:

- The headline
- Features of the product
- Testimonials or a case study
- And sometimes a call to action (a button encouraging you to learn more or to buy something)

Let's add those to our page.

Adding content to a landing page

Now that we have an empty page ready to go, we need to add some content to it. With WordPress's new block interface, there's a lot of potential content that we can add. Let's start by adding a few different types of content to our page. You can add any content you want to your page, but I'm going to focus on visual content, in order to draw our reader's eye to the page.

Let's start with a cover image, which we can do with a few simple steps:

1. On the **Edit** page screen for your landing page, click the + button to add a new block.
2. Add a **Cover** block, as shown in the following screenshot:

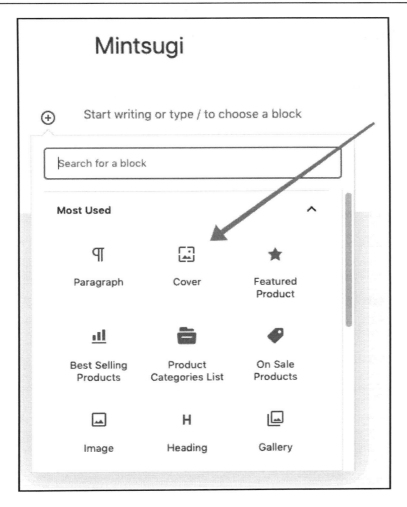

3. Upload an image that's a visual representation of the product.
4. Add a headline by selecting the **Heading** option, as shown in the previous image.
5. If you're using Astra, you can check **Disable Title** under **Astra Settings** in the sidebar in order to hide the default title. In many cases, this is fine, as long as we described the page in the cover image.

Here's what that looks like on the **Edit** page:

And here's what it looks like on the frontend:

A strong image with a headline is a great start to building an effective landing page. Let's look into adding some features to the page. Follow these steps:

1. On the **Edit** page, add a **New Paragraph** block, and add a short description of the game.
2. Then add a **Pull Quote** block and add the quote.
3. Add a **Heading** block.
4. Add **Media** and **Text** blocks. As you add these blocks and fill them with content, feel free to alternate where the images are. It's very common to alternate images from left to right.
5. Add a **Video** block, and add a bit more information about your product.
6. Add a **Quote** block with some social proof that your product is actually good.
7. Save/update your page.

And it should look something like what is shown in the following image:

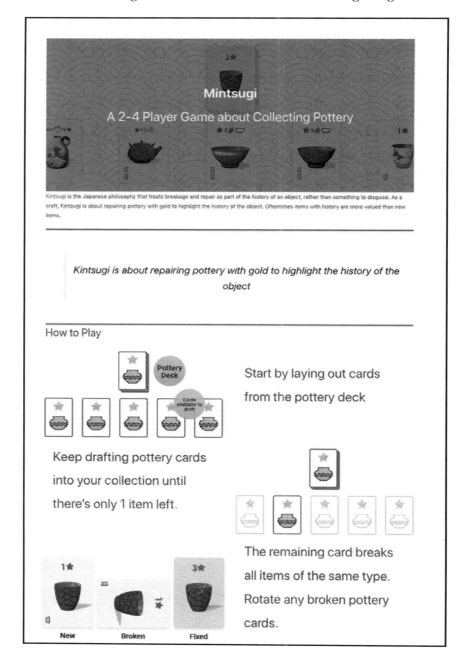

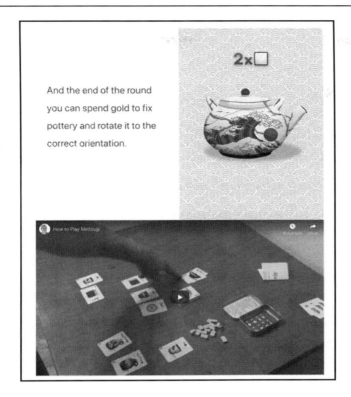

The new blocks in WordPress 5.0 are incredibly powerful for creating landing pages. I created this in less than 10 minutes with a handful of images. If you spend the time to craft a well-honed marketing message, and spend a little more time tweaking the page design itself, you can create an absolutely gorgeous landing page for a product.

Now that we have an attractive landing page that clearly explains our product and entices users to buy it we can now look at how to add e-commerce functionality to a landing page.

Adding e-commerce to a landing page

Our landing page is looking pretty good. Now that we've done a good job of showing off our awesome product with different types of content, we just need to give viewers a way to purchase the product. There are a couple of ways to do this: we can use the featured product block, we can add an **Add to cart** button to the page, or we could also use the One Page Checkout extension.

Let's start with the easiest method, which is adding a featured product block. Then we'll look into adding an **Add to cart** button directly to the page.

Adding a featured product

Before we can let users add a product to their cart, we have to add the product to our store. We don't have to add every single field, but we need to add enough in order to display useful information on the landing page.

Let's add the product first. Follow these steps:

1. Under **Products**, navigate to **Add New** as in the following screenshot:

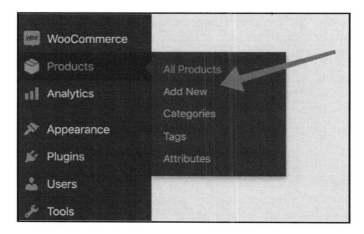

We need to fill the following fields for our products:

- **Add a title**
- **Add a product image**
- **Add a description**
- **Set a price**

2. Save the product.

Now, on our landing page, we can add a **Featured Product** block. To add one, follow these steps:

1. Add a new **Featured Product** block.
2. Search for the product that we just added, as shown in the following image:

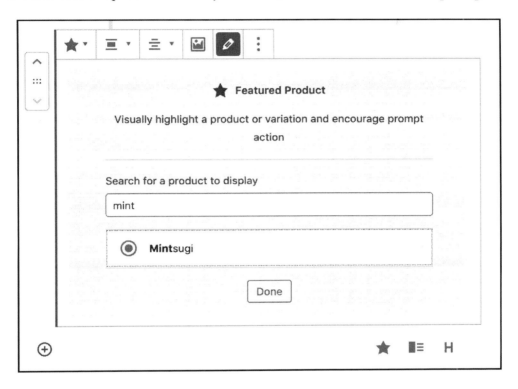

3. You can select the featured product to tweak the overlay and button colors, and it should look something like this on the frontend:

This certainly works, and it is a nice way to break up large sections of text. You can add a few different call-to-actions throughout the page, for example, a button. As soon as someone is convinced that this is the right product for them, they'll click the button and go to the product page, where they can add the product to their cart.

Adding an add-to-cart button

If you want to take what we've already done, and just have a button instead of a whole featured product block, you can do so by creating an add-to-cart button.

We can do this by creating a magic URL that automatically adds a product to the cart and loads the cart page. It will look something like this: `https://yourstore.com/cart/?add-to-cart={{product-id}}`

You just need to replace the dummy domain with your domain and add the product ID to the URL. Let's start by finding the product ID.

Finding the product ID

We can find a product ID by going to our list of products in our Wordpress admin. If you hover over the product, you'll be able to see an ID number. This is shown in the following image:

Next up, we can add our button.

Adding the button

Once we have our ID, we can our button. On the **Edit Page** screen for our landing page do the following:

1. Add a new block as shown in the following screenshot. In our case, the block that we are adding is a **Button**:

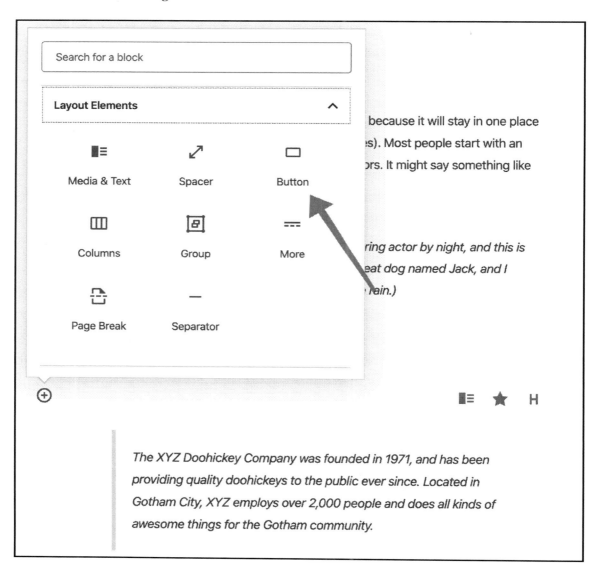

2. Select the **Button** block.

3. Enter text for the button. I suggest **Add to cart**, followed by the price.

4. For the link, add `https://yourstore.com/cart/?add-to-cart={{product-id}}`. Of course, replace the domain with your own domain and add your product ID.

5. Save your page.

If anyone clicks the button they should land on the cart page with the product already in their cart. This can be seen in the following image, which has been taken from my site:

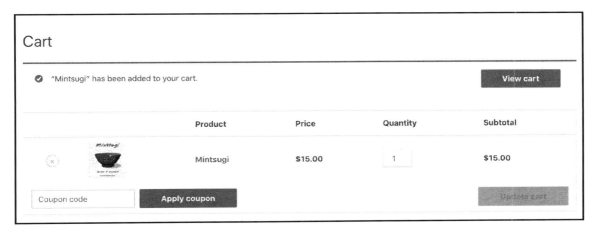

Now that we have a landing page, and users can add a product to their cart, we can share it with the world and get sales. That's fantastic news!

Building a landing page is great, but we can take it a step further by experimenting with the page. In the web development world, this is usually called A/B testing, since we're testing if version A is better or worse than version B.

A/B test everything

Now that we have everything set up, it's worth testing if it works. Oftentimes, when you launch a new product, you don't know what resonates the most with your audience. Sometimes you have a few guesses and you want to test them.

We can set up an A/B test, where certain users see one version of the landing page and other users see the second version. We can then compare which group had a higher conversion rate, and figure out which marketing message resonates with our audience.

Let's install some software that will help us to create alternative versions of pages, as well as monitor how successful they are. We'll install the software, set up the test, and then measure the results.

Install the Simple Page Tester plugin

The first thing that we have to do is install A/B testing software. There's a lot of really good A/B testing software for larger companies that have the budget to do really good testing, but for smaller WordPress companies I recommend Simple Page Tester (`https://wordpress.org/plugins/simple-page-tester/`).

It's free and is built on top of WordPress. Let's install it:

1. On your admin dashboard, go to **Plugins** | **Add New**.
2. Search for **Simple Page Tester**:

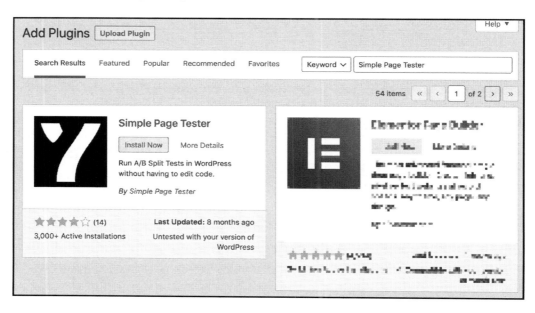

3. Install and activate the plugin.

Now that we have it installed, we can start an experiment.

Set up an experiment

Now that we have our plugin ready to go, we can set up an experiment. On the admin dashboard, there's a new menu item called **Split Tests**. However, it's actually easier to start an experiment from the **Edit** page. Follow these steps:

1. Navigate to your landing page in the admin.
2. You'll see a new menu, which we can see in this screenshot:

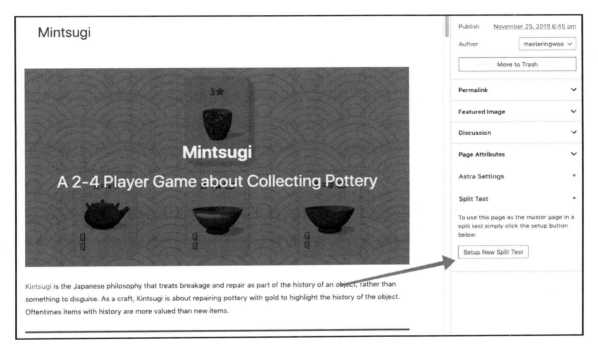

3. Click **Setup New Split Test**, which determines your **master** page.

4. From here, we need to create a variation on this page. In the new popup, select **Duplicate Master Page**, which we can see here:

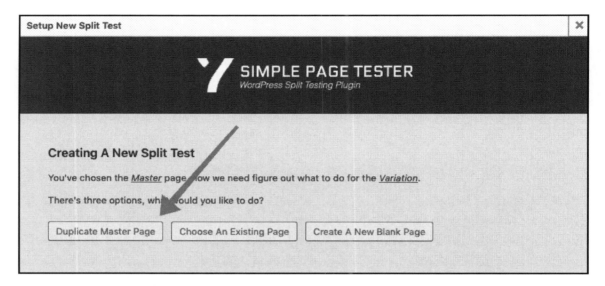

5. Now, we have two duplicated pages, and the split test is ready to go. However, we still need to actually change the variation page. On the page, you can see both pages and edit either one. Under **Variation**, select **Edit Page**, which we can see here:

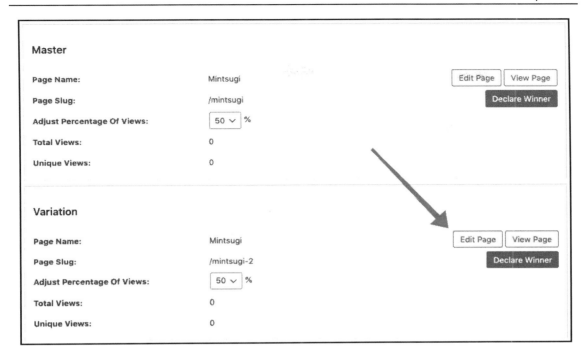

From here, you can make as many changes to the variation as you like. Some people like to change a tiny thing, such as a headline, whereas others like to make sweeping changes. The more visitors that you have, the smaller the changes you can make and still notice the different effects.

If you are only going to get a couple of hundred visitors to the pages, I recommend making sweeping changes so that you'll be able to do something with your numbers. If you make subtle changes, you probably won't be able to see a difference.

Measuring results

There's no point in setting up an experiment if you can't see the results. There are two ways to measure the results:

- Get the premium version of Simple Page Tester and see the results on your dashboard.
- Use the free version of Simple Page Tester and see the results in Google Analytics.

The plugin developers provide a nice guide to help you: get started with goal tracking in Google Analytics (`https://simplepagetester.com/articles/setup-goals-split-test-tracking/`).

Once you've compared the results and you're pretty sure about your numbers, you can declare a winner and the plugin will make that page the new master page, and delete the old page. Now, all of your visitors will see the winning page.

Summary

Landing pages are an incredibly important tool for marketing campaigns. Now that you've finished this chapter, you should know how you can build landing pages, how to add e-commerce functionality to landing pages, and how to experiment with landing pages in order to determine the layout that works best for your audience. Now that you know how to do this, you can promote and effectively sell your products.

In the next chapter, we'll look into creating and customizing WooCommerce plugins.

13
Creating Plugins for WooCommerce

Ultimately, WooCommerce is a flexible platform not because of the existing plugins but because you can code your own plugin. You can customize every single line of WordPress and WooCommerce, which means you can literally change anything – it's incredibly powerful.

Becoming a WooCommerce developer could be its own series of books, but we will start by looking at how you can customize a WooCommerce plugin.

 This chapter will require you to write code. You should be familiar with PHP code and object-oriented programming to get the most out of this chapter.

We're going to build a basic WooCommerce plugin, look into building integration with WooCommerce, and then customize the edit product page.

The following topics will be covered in this chapter:

- Building a basic WooCommerce plugin
- Customizing order statuses
- Building a settings page with WooCommerce

By the end of this chapter, you should know the basics of building a plugin to customize WooCommerce.

First, we need to build a basic WooCommerce plugin.

Technical requirements

The code files for this chapter can be found on the following GitHub repository: https://github.com/PacktPublishing/Mastering-WooCommerce-4

Building a basic WooCommerce plugin

To get started, we want to build a plugin that will run when WooCommerce is activated on a site. If WooCommerce is not active, we don't want our plugin to run, because that's a waste of processing power.

We're going to create a plugin and then we'll configure it to only load when WooCommerce is active. We need to start by creating a plugin file.

Creating a plugin

To get started, we need to create the plugin files. Plugins are typically stored in the WordPress filesystem under `wp-content/plugins/{your-plugin}`.

There are two ways of creating plugin files:

- Use a single plugin file that contains the entire plugin.
- Use a folder with multiple plugin files.

Almost all modern plugins use multiple files, so we're going to create a folder for our plugin. Follow the steps given here:

1. Under `/wp-content/plugins/`, add a folder for your plugin. I'm going to call mine `woocommerce-example-plugin`:

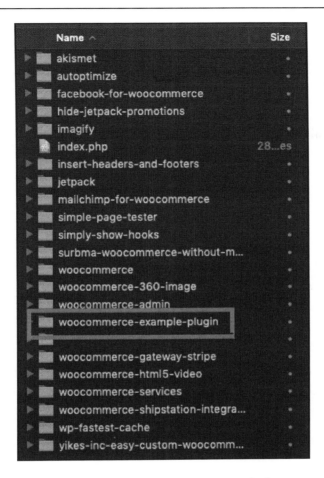

Name ^	Size
▶ akismet	•
▶ autoptimize	•
▶ facebook-for-woocommerce	•
▶ hide-jetpack-promotions	•
▶ imagify	•
index.php	28...es
▶ insert-headers-and-footers	•
▶ jetpack	•
▶ mailchimp-for-woocommerce	•
▶ simple-page-tester	•
▶ simply-show-hooks	•
▶ surbma-woocommerce-without-m...	•
▶ woocommerce	•
▶ woocommerce-360-image	•
▶ woocommerce-admin	•
woocommerce-example-plugin	•
	•
▶ woocommerce-gateway-stripe	•
▶ woocommerce-html5-video	•
▶ woocommerce-services	•
▶ woocommerce-shipstation-integra...	•
▶ wp-fastest-cache	•
▶ yikes-inc-easy-custom-woocomm...	•

2. Navigate inside of that folder and create a file with the same name. I'll call mine `woocommerce-example-plugin.php`. This will be the main file for the plugin.

3. Open up your main plugin file in a code editor such as Sublime Text, Atom, or Notepad ++.

4. Add the following plugin header information (`https://developer.wordpress.org/plugins/plugin-basics/header-requirements/`). This information is displayed in your WordPress backend:

```php
<?php
/*
Plugin Name: WooCommerce Example Plugin
Plugin URI: http://speakinginbytes.com
Description: A wrapper plugin for our custom WooCommerce
functionality
```

```
Version: 1.0
Author: Patrick Rauland
Author URI: http://speakinginbytes.com
License: GPL2
License URI: https://www.gnu.org/licenses/gpl-2.0.html
Text Domain: woocommerce-example-plugin
Domain Path: /languages
*/
```

5. Save the file.

If we stopped right now we'd have a completely valid plugin that would show up in the backend of WordPress, but it wouldn't do anything. Let's program our plugin so it only runs when WooCommerce is active.

Checking if WooCommerce is active

We're going to build our plugin from the inside out. We're going to build a class that could do anything and then we're going to build conditions such as checking to make sure WooCommerce is active around the core functionality so it only runs when those conditions are true. Follow these steps:

1. Let's create an empty plugin class. Add the following just beneath the plugin header:

```
class WC_Example{
  public function __construct(){
  }
}
$GLOBALS['wc_example'] = new WC_Example();
```

The line of code with $GLOBALS['wc_example'] = new WC_Example(); is useful when you want to allow another plugin to refer to your plugin, but it isn't required.

2. Whenever you add classes, you should make sure there isn't an existing class name. Let's add this condition around the class:

```
// only run if there's no other class with this name

if ( ! class_exists('WC_Example')){
  ((our existing code))
```

3. Let's check to make sure WooCommerce is active. Add the following code around our existing code:

```
// Check to make sure WooCommerce is active
if ( in_array( 'woocommerce/woocommerce.php',
  apply_filters('active_plugins', get_option('active_plugins'))))
{
 ((our existing code))
 }
```

By the end, the code should look like this:

```
<?php
/*
Plugin Name: WooCommerce Example Plugin
Plugin URI: http://speakinginbytes.com
Description: A wrapper plugin for our custom WooCommerce
functionality
Version: 1.0
Author: Patrick Rauland
Author URI: http://speakinginbytes.com
License: GPL2
License URI: https://www.gnu.org/licenses/gpl-2.0.html
Text Domain: woocommerce-example-plugin
Domain Path: /languages
*/
// Check to make sure WooCommerce is active
if ( in_array( 'woocommerce/woocommerce.php',
apply_filters('active_plugins',
get_option('active_plugins')))) {
// only run if there's no other class with this name
if ( ! class_exists('WC_Example')){
class WC_Example{
public function __construct(){
}
}
$GLOBALS['wc_example'] = new WC_Example();
}
}
```

Any code you add to the constructor function will only run when WooCommerce is active. This is one of the best ways to start writing your own WooCommerce plugins, since it prevents a lot of potential problems.

Now that we know how to write a plugin that works well with WooCommerce and prevents other problems, we can write specific functionality to customize our store.

Customizing order statuses

WooCommerce uses order statuses to track the state of orders. WooCommerce includes several different order statuses including the following:

- Completed
- Processing
- Pending payment
- On hold
- Refunded
- Canceled
- Failed

But some shops may need more order statuses. You might need a "Building" status to indicate that you started building the order. You can easily add a custom order status yourself with some custom code. We're going to start with our WooCommerce Example plugin and then we're going to register a post status and add it to WooCommerce.

Using the WooCommerce Example plugin

We can start by using the example plugin we created earlier in this chapter.

We'll copy the example code, and then we should change the name of the class from `WC_Example` to `WC_Building_Order_Status`, since this describes what this plugin will do. Here's the code:

```
// Check to make sure WooCommerce is active
 if ( in_array( 'woocommerce/woocommerce.php',
  apply_filters('active_plugins',
   get_option('active_plugins')))) {
  // only run if there's no other class with this name
  if ( ! class_exists('WC_Building_Order_Status')){
    class WC_Building_Order_Status{
      public function __construct(){
       }
    }
   $GLOBALS['wc_building_order_status'] = new WC_Building_Order_Status();
   }
 }
```

We can also add the following code to class to the list of global variables. This will help other plugins interact with ours. It is purely optional, so you could skip this, but it is a good practice to do so.
`$GLOBALS['wc_building_order_status'] = new WC_Building_Order_Status();`

Now we can call two functions from that constructor. We're going to have to add a new post status and then tell WooCommerce where that new post status should show up. We're going to write code to call specific functions that we'll write later.

Add the following to your constructor:

```
// register the new post status
register_building_order_status();

// add to list of WooCommerce order statuses
add_filter( 'wc_order_statuses', 'add_building_to_order_statuses' );
```

Now that we've called two functions, we need to write both of them.

Registering a post status and adding it to WooCommerce

The first function we called should register a post status. Remember, this is what tracks the status of an order. So we need to add a new post status so we can select it from a dropdown.

This is pretty easy to do if you read through the documentation on the WordPress website about post statuses, available at `https://developer.wordpress.org/reference/functions/register_post_status/`. It only takes a few lines, as you can see here:

```
function register_building_order_status() {
    register_post_status( 'wc-building', array(
        'label' => 'Building',
        'public' => true,
        'exclude_from_search' => false,
        'show_in_admin_all_list' => true,
        'show_in_admin_status_list' => true,
        'label_count' => _n_noop( 'Building <span class="count">(%s)</span>',
        'Building <span class="count">(%s)</span>' )
    ) );
}
```

With this function, we created a new post status called Building and we also hid it from searches and from a few other areas in your WordPress site. Your site doesn't know when or where it should show that post status.

Now we need to tell WooCommerce when to display this new order status. We'll loop through each of the existing order statuses in WooCommerce and add our new order status right after wc-processing, which is the Processing status:

```
function add_building_to_order_statuses( $order_statuses ) {
  $new_order_statuses = array();
  // add new order status after processing
   foreach ( $order_statuses as $key => $status ) {
    $new_order_statuses[ $key ] = $status;
    if ( 'wc-processing' === $key ) {
       $new_order_statuses['wc-building'] = 'Building';
     }
   }
  return $new_order_statuses;
}
```

With this code, we're looping through all of the order statuses. If we find one called wc-processing, we add a new order status called Building.

When you're done, save your files, make sure your plugin is activated in the backend, and then open up an order. You should see your new order status, as we can see in the following screenshot:

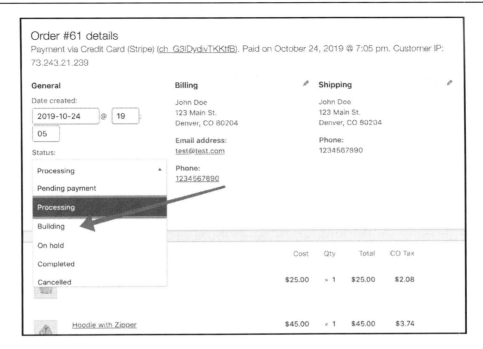

Now we can change any order to the **Building** status. This will help us track the status of orders. In this example, we added one order status, but you could add as many as you wanted to help you track your orders.

Next up, we will look at building integration with WooCommerce.

Building a settings page with WooCommerce

When you're building your own plugin, you'll very likely have to build a settings page. There's a lot to building a settings page from scratch. But if you are just building an integration, WooCommerce created some technology that makes it easier for you to add your own settings screen.

We're going to cover some of the coding decisions in the WooCommerce `Integration` class. If you want, you can see the finished code at `https://github.com/woogists/woocommerce-integration-demo`.

We can see that one of the plugins we looked at earlier in this book takes advantage of the Integration class, which we can see in the following screenshot:

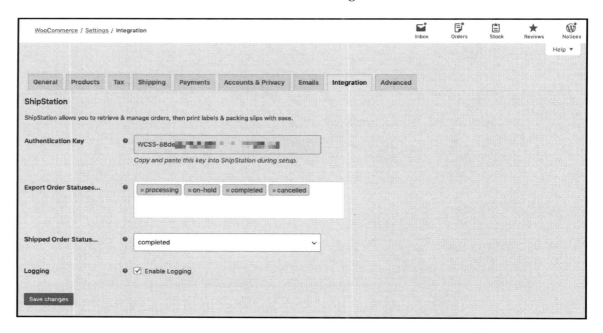

 We're not going to explain every single line. But we are going to cover the essential lines and why you need them.

Let's build our own settings page using the Integration class. We'll start by creating the main file.

Creating the main integration file

The main integration file will activate all other functionality in the Integration class. So let's start with that. Follow the steps given here:

1. Let's create a new plugin folder in /wp-content/plugins/. We can call it woocommerce-integration-demo.
2. Create woocommerce-integration-demo.php

3. Open that file.

4. Paste in the following plugin header:

```php
<?php
/**
 * Plugin Name: WooCommerce Integration Demo
 * Plugin URI: https://github.com/BFTrick/woocommerce-
    integration-demo
 * Description: A plugin demonstrating how to add
    a new WooCommerce integration.
 * Author: Patrick Rauland
 * Author URI: http://speakinginbytes.com/
 * Version: 1.0

 */
```

5. Now we have the real work to do. Let's first check if the WooCommerce `Integration` class exists. If it does, we can include it and then call our own function to register our own integration:

```php
// Checks if WooCommerce is installed.
if ( class_exists( 'WC_Integration' ) ) {
  // Include our integration class.
  include_once 'includes/class-wc-integration
   -demo-integration.php';
  // Register the integration.
  add_filter( 'woocommerce_integrations',
   array( $this, 'add_integration' ) );
} else {
  // throw an admin error if you like
}
```

6. We called a function (`add_integration`) to register our own function. We need to tell WooCommerce what to do with this file. We can add our integration to the list of integrations that WooCommerce automatically loads. Let's add the name of our integration to the array of integrations:

```php
/**
 * Add a new integration to WooCommerce.
 */
public function add_integration( $integrations ) {
    $integrations[] = 'WC_Integration_Demo_Integration';
    return $integrations;
}
```

That's pretty much it for this first file. We loaded our own integration file and told WooCommerce to add it to the list of integrations.

When we're done, it should look like this:

```php
<?php
/**
 * Plugin Name: WooCommerce Integration Demo
 * Plugin URI: https://github.com/BFTrick/woocommerce-
   integration-demo
 * Description: A plugin demonstrating how to add
   a new WooCommerce integration.
 * Author: Patrick Rauland
 * Author URI: http://speakinginbytes.com/
 * Version: 1.0
 */

if ( ! class_exists( 'WC_Integration_Demo' ) ) :

class WC_Integration_Demo {
  /**
   * Construct the plugin.
   */
  public function __construct() {
    add_action( 'plugins_loaded', array( $this, 'init' ) );
  }
  /**
   * Initialize the plugin.
   */
  public function init() {
   // Checks if WooCommerce is installed.
    if ( class_exists( 'WC_Integration' ) ) {
      // Include our integration class.
      include_once 'includes/class-wc-integration
        -demo-integration.php';
   // Register the integration.
      add_filter( 'woocommerce_integrations',
       array( $this, 'add_integration' ) );
    } else {
      // throw an admin error if you like
    }
  }
  /**
   * Add a new integration to WooCommerce.
   */
  public function add_integration( $integrations ) {
    $integrations[] = 'WC_Integration_Demo_Integration';
    return $integrations;
```

```
    }
  }
  $WC_Integration_Demo = new WC_Integration_Demo( __FILE__ );
  endif;
```

The preceding code creates the basics of our integration and tells WooCommerce to load our integration. Now we need to actually create our own integration file, which will specify exactly what settings we need.

Creating the Integration child class

The way we're creating our settings page is by taking advantage of a concept in programming called *inheritance*. Inheritance means we're using a child class that inherits programming from the parent class. Basically, WooCommerce wrote the parent `Integration` class and we're going to write a child class that will automatically have certain things defined, which will save us dozens of hours of coding.

There are two important pieces of the `Integration` child class. The first part is the constructor and the second is where we define our settings. Let's look at the constructor first.

Creating a constructor

The constructor is where we declare all of our integration information, load our settings, and add our own variables that the user can interact with. Follow these steps:

1. Let's start with an empty constructor:

```
/**
 * Init and hook in the integration.
 */
public function __construct() {
  global $woocommerce;
  }
```

2. Now let's configure some integration settings. Add the following code to your constructor right after `global $woocommerce`:

```
$this->id = 'integration-demo';
$this->method_title = __( 'Integration Demo', 'woocommerce-
integration-demo' );
$this->method_description = __( 'An integration demo to show you
how easy it is to extend WooCommerce.',
'woocommerce-integration-demo' );
```

3. The rest of the constructor is for our settings. We need to load the settings, add fields, process our options, and sanitize the options. Add the following after our previous code:

```
// Load the settings.
$this->init_form_fields();
$this->init_settings();
// Define user set variables.
$this->api_key = $this->get_option( 'api_key' );
$this->debug = $this->get_option( 'debug' );
// Actions.
add_action( 'woocommerce_update_options_integration_' . $this->id,
array( $this, 'process_admin_options' ) );
// Filters.
add_filter( 'woocommerce_settings_api_sanitized_fields_' .
$this->id, array( $this, 'sanitize_settings' ) );
```

Don't worry about the user-set variables. We'll cover that in the next section.

The following code shows the finished constructor:

```
/**
 * Init and hook in the integration.
 */
public function __construct() {
  global $woocommerce;
  $this->id = 'integration-demo';
  $this->method_title = __( 'Integration Demo',
    'woocommerce-integration-demo' );
  $this->method_description = __( 'An integration demo to
    show you how easy it is to extend WooCommerce.',
    'woocommerce-integration-demo' );
  // Load the settings.
  $this->init_form_fields();
  $this->init_settings();
  // Define user set variables.
  $this->api_key = $this->get_option( 'api_key' );
  $this->debug = $this->get_option( 'debug' );
```

```
// Actions.
add_action( 'woocommerce_update_options_integration_' .
  $this->id, array( $this, 'process_admin_options' ) );
// Filters.
add_filter( 'woocommerce_settings_api_sanitized_fields_' .
  $this->id, array( $this, 'sanitize_settings' ) );
}
```

The preceding code tells WooCommerce the title, description, and settings fields we want to see on the page. Now that we told WooCommerce, we want settings, we have to define which settings. Let's write our field settings.

Adding field settings

Now that we have our basic integration setup, we need to add our fields. So far, everything we've written will work for just about any integration. Now we're going to write code for the specific settings our integration needs. Follow these steps:

1. Let's start with a function to create the fields:

```
/**
 * Initialize integration settings form fields.
 *
 * @return void
 */
public function init_form_fields() {
    }
```

2. Now we can add the settings to this function. Let's add one setting first. Add a field for our API key. We're going to create an array called `form_fields` and add all of our fields to that array:

```
$this->form_fields = array(
    'api_key' => array(
      'title' => __( 'API Key', 'woocommerce-integration-demo' ),
      'type' => 'text',
      'description' => __( 'Enter with your API Key.
        You can find this in "User Profile" drop-down
          (top right corner) >
          API Keys.', 'woocommerce-integration-demo' ),
      'desc_tip' => true,
      'default' => ''
    ),
  );
```

The preceding code is for an API key. The three important fields are as follows:

- `title`: The name of the field.
- `type`: It's a text field (as opposed to a paragraph or number input).
- `description`: This shows up next to the text field to explain what it is to the user.

Now that we know how to add one field, you can add the rest of our fields. WooCommerce has a whole section in the documentation about these fields. If you want to know the types of fields you can display and what each setting means, read through their documentation at `https://docs.woocommerce.com/document/implementing-wc-integration/#section-3`.

The following code shows the complete array when you finish adding fields:

```
$this->form_fields = array(
    'api_key' => array(
        'title' => __( 'API Key', 'woocommerce-integration-demo' ),
        'type' => 'text',
        'description' => __( 'Enter with your API Key.
        You can find this in "User Profile" drop-down (top right corner) >
        API Keys.', 'woocommerce-integration-demo' ),
        'desc_tip' => true,
        'default' => ''
    ),
    'debug' => array(
        'title' => __( 'Debug Log', 'woocommerce-integration-demo' ),
        'type' => 'checkbox',
        'label' => __( 'Enable logging', 'woocommerce-integration-demo' ),
        'default' => 'no',
        'description' => __( 'Log events such as API requests',
        'woocommerce-integration-demo' ),

    ),
    'customize_button' => array(
        'title' => __( 'Customize!', 'woocommerce-integration-demo' ),
        'type' => 'button',
        'custom_attributes' => array(
        'onclick' => "location.href='http://www.woothemes.com'",

    ),
        'description' => __( 'Customize your settings by going
        to the integration site directly.',
        'woocommerce-integration-demo' ),
        'desc_tip' => true,
    )
);
```

The preceding code is similar to the code for one settings field. I wanted to show you what it looks like when you have multiple fields. Notice the different field types such as `button` and `checkbox`.

When we're done, this function should look like the following:

```
/**
 * Initialize integration settings form fields.
 *
 * @return void
 */
public function init_form_fields() {
  $this->form_fields = array(
    'api_key' => array(
      'title' => __( 'API Key', 'woocommerce-integration-demo' ),
      'type' => 'text',
      'description' => __( 'Enter with your API Key.
      You can find this in "User Profile" drop-down (top right corner) >
      API Keys.', 'woocommerce-integration-demo' ),
      'desc_tip' => true,
      'default' => ''
    ),
    'debug' => array(
      'title' => __( 'Debug Log', 'woocommerce-integration-demo' ),
      'type' => 'checkbox',
      'label' => __( 'Enable logging', 'woocommerce-integration-demo' ),
      'default' => 'no',
      'description' => __( 'Log events such as API requests',
      'woocommerce-integration-demo' ),
    ),
    'customize_button' => array(
      'title' => __( 'Customize!', 'woocommerce-integration-demo' ),
      'type' => 'button',
      'custom_attributes' => array(
      'onclick' => "location.href='http://www.woothemes.com'",
    ),
      'description' => __( 'Customize your settings by going
      to the integration site directly.',
      'woocommerce-integration-demo' ),
      'desc_tip' => true,
    )
  );
}
```

The preceding block shows what our code looks like when all of the settings fields are added to the `init_form_fields` method.

When you're all done it and you load the `Integrations` page, it will look something like the following screenshot:

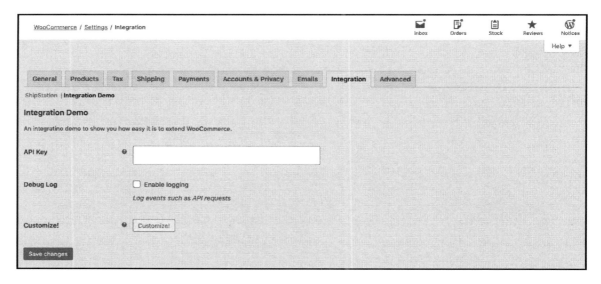

This is some of the simplest code I can show you to customize WooCommerce. But it's still pretty complex for new coders. This code might take a seasoned developer an hour or more to figure out and customize to suit their needs. So don't worry if it takes you a while to understand. I highly recommend that you read through the documentation, available at `https://docs.woocommerce.com/document/implementing-wc-integration/` so you can fully understand it.

Summary

WooCommerce is an incredibly open system where you can do just about anything. We covered some simple tutorials in this chapter to give you a taste of what you can do. You should now know how to build a plugin that only works when WooCommerce is active, how to customize order statuses, and how to build an integration with another service.

You've taken these first steps; now you can learn a lot more, and eventually become a WooCommerce plugin developer.

Other Books You May Enjoy

If you enjoyed this book, you may be interested in these other books by Packt:

WordPress 5 Cookbook
Rakhitha Nimesh Ratnayake

ISBN: 978-1-83898-650-6

- Install and customize WordPress themes and plugins for building websites
- Develop modern web designs without the need to write any code
- Explore the new Gutenberg content editor introduced in WordPress 5 (Bebo)
- Use the existing WordPress plugins to add custom features and monetize your website
- Improve user interaction and accessibility for your website with simple tricks
- Discover powerful techniques for maintaining and securing your websites
- Extend built-in WordPress features for advanced website management

WordPress 5 Complete - Seventh Edition
Karol Król

ISBN: 978-1-78953-201-2

- Learn to adapt your plugin with the Gutenberg editor
- Create content that is optimized for publication on the web
- Craft great looking pages and posts with the use of block editor
- Structure your web pages in an accessible and clear way
- Install and work with plugins and themes
- Customize the design of your website
- Upload multimedia content, such as images, audio, and video easily and effectively
- Develop your own WordPress plugins and themes
- Use WordPress to build websites that serve purposes other than blogs

Leave a review - let other readers know what you think

Please share your thoughts on this book with others by leaving a review on the site that you bought it from. If you purchased the book from Amazon, please leave us an honest review on this book's Amazon page. This is vital so that other potential readers can see and use your unbiased opinion to make purchasing decisions, we can understand what our customers think about our products, and our authors can see your feedback on the title that they have worked with Packt to create. It will only take a few minutes of your time, but is valuable to other potential customers, our authors, and Packt. Thank you!

Index

D

data in-store
  syncing 161
data online
  syncing 161
data
  syncing, manually 162
database
  using 161
Dear Systems
  about 142, 143, 144
  URL 141
descriptions
  writing, for product categories 73, 74
digital products 47
downloadable product
  about 48
  configuring 48
downloads
  accessing 51

E

e-commerce functionality
  testing, with publicly accessible URL 9, 10
e-commerce
  adding, to long-form landing page 281
  issues 8
  keywords, researching for 93
emails
  sending 164, 165
Enterprise Resource Planning (ERP) system
  about 140
  finding 141
  using 144

F

files
  migrating 9
fold 220
free traffic
  acquiring 93

G

Google
  XML sitemap, submitting to 105, 106
grouped products 52, 53, 54
GTMetrix
  periodic testing, setting up 202, 203, 204
  using 194, 195, 196

H

hook visualizers
  installing 238, 239, 240, 241
hooks
  code for actions, browsing 241, 242
  viewing, on frontend 236, 238
HTACCESS
  caching, configuring via 219

I

image filenames
  SEO tip 33
images
  about 31
  lazy loading, with Jetpack 222, 223
  optimizing 208
  optimizing, with bulk updater 213, 215, 216
  optimizing, with Imagify 211, 212, 213
  optimizing, with Jetpack 208, 209, 210
Imagify
  used, for optimizing images 211, 212, 213
inheritance 305
Integration child class
  constructor, creating 305, 307
  field settings, adding 307, 308, 309, 310

J

JavaScript resources
  minifying 204
Jetpack Without Promotions 11
Jetpack
  used, for lazy loading images 222, 223
  used, for optimizing images 208, 209, 210

Printed in Poland
by Amazon Fulfillment
Poland Sp. z o.o., Wrocław

57053127R00188